# ANYTHING TO DECLARE?

Maurice Hennequin
and Pierre Véber
translated by
Laurence Senelick

BROADWAY PLAY PUBLISHING INC
New York
www.broadwayplaypublishing.com
info@broadwayplaypublishing.com

ANYTHING TO DECLARE?
© Copyright 1997 by Laurence Senelick

All rights reserved. This work is fully protected under the copyright laws of the United States of America. No part of this publication may be photocopied, reproduced, stored in a retrieval system, or transmitted, in any form or by any means, electronic, mechanical, recording, or otherwise, without the prior permission of the publisher. Additional copies of this play are available from the publisher.

Written permission is required for live performance of any sort. This includes readings, cuttings, scenes, and excerpts. For amateur and stock performances, please contact Broadway Play Publishing Inc. For all other rights please contact the translator c/o Department of Drama, Tufts University, Medford MA 02155..

Book design: Marie Donovan
Page make-up: Adobe Indesign
Typeface: Palatino

VOUS N'AVEZ RIEN À DECLARER? was first produced at the Théâtre des Nouveautés, Paris, 6 October 1906

# CHARACTERS & SETTING

DUPONT, *a magistrate*
MADAME DUPONT, *his wife*
LISE, *their younger daughter*
PAULETTE DE TRIVELIN, *their elder daughter*
ROBERT DE TRIVELIN, PAULETTE'*s husband*
LA BAULE, PAULETTE'*s former suitor*
COUZAN, *a friend of the* DUPONT *family*
FRONTIGNAC, *from North Africa*
GONTRAN DES BARBETTES, LISE'*s fiancé*
ERNESTINE, *the* DUPONTS' *maid*
ZÉZÉ, *a courtesan*
MARIETTE, *her maid*
GOLD MEDAL, *an award-winning painter*
A POLICE INSPECTOR
*Two* POLICEMEN

*Translator's note: In* ACT TWO, *the roles of the* POLICE INSPECTOR *and the* POLICEMEN *may be doubled by the actors playing* COUZAN, GONTRAN, *and* LA BAULE. MARIETTE *may also be doubled by the actress playing* LISE, PAULETTE, *or* ERNESTINE.

*Paris, about 1905. The first and third acts at the* DUPONTS' *apartment, the second act at* ZÉZÉ's *flat.*

## ACT ONE

*(A drawing room in the* Duponts' *apartment. Comfortable expensive furnishings. Upstage, an entrance door. Doors L and R on the side walls. Two other doors D R and D L. A fireplace between the two doors R. At R, a table between a sofa R and a chair L. At L, an easy chair, to its R an ottoman. L of the U door, a breakfront against the wall. Paintings, chairs, etc. R of the U door, a bell-buzzer. L of the D R door, a light-switch. On the table, a tray with a coffee urn, cups, a bottle of cognac, a sugar bowl, liqueur glasses, etc.)*

LISE: *(Speaking into the wings)* All right, mama, I'll see to the coffee. *(She heads for the table.)*

GONTRAN: *(Entering D L)* Psst! Mademoiselle Lise!

LISE: Monsieur Gontran! Are you following me?

GONTRAN: Your mother didn't see me leave, neither did your father... And after all, I am engaged to you.

LISE: That won't make any difference to mama when she finds out you're missing.

GONTRAN: Is she really that strict?

LISE: Is she! When my sister Paulette and Monsieur de Trivelin were engaged, she watched them like a hawk. She never left them alone for a second.

GONTRAN: Which didn't keep them from kissing in corners, I'm sure.

LISE: Never! ...Paulette was too naive and shy. Just think! They'll be back from their honeymoon in an hour!

GONTRAN: You seem awfully eager to see your sister.

LISE: And question her.

GONTRAN: Question her? What about?

LISE: Oh...lots of things... Her trip, since you and I will be taking the same one! *(She crosses D R.)*

GONTRAN: True enough! Another month of waiting! Ah! Lise darling! Lise dearest! *(He moves to kiss her.)*

LISE: Watch out! Every time you kiss me somebody walks in.

GONTRAN: Don't be silly...

(GONTRAN *kisses* LISE. ERNESTINE *enters U C.*)

ERNESTINE: Mademoiselle... Oh!

LISE: *(Quickly, as if* GONTRAN *were removing a pin)* There's a pin sticking in me. Back here, in my neck... Did you get it?

GONTRAN: Here it is!

ERNESTINE: *(Aside)* A likely story!

LISE: What is it, Ernestine?

ERNESTINE: It's Monsieur La Baule, mademoiselle!

LISE: Oh, drat!

GONTRAN: Your sister's ex-fiancé?

LISE: Yes, my parents promised to give her to him, but Paulette fell madly in love with De Trivelin...so Papa went back on his word to poor La Baule.

GONTRAN: And he keeps coming here anyway?

LISE: Oh, he got in the habit of calling on us twice a week... We see him because we feel sorry for him...

# ACT ONE

And he's such a bore... As soon as anybody mentions Paulette, he starts crying. Let's go back to the dining room.

ERNESTINE: Shall I show in Monsieur La Baule?

LISE: *(Exiting D L with* GONTRAN*)* All right, and keep him company.

ERNESTINE: *(Opening the door U C)* Come in, Monsieur La Baule.

LA BAULE: *(Entering bouquet in hand)* Thank you, Ernestine!

ERNESTINE: Another bouquet?

LA BAULE: *(Dolefully)* In the old days whenever I called, I would bring my bride-to-be a bouquet. I continue to bring bouquets. I have made a religion of my sad memories!

ERNESTINE: Monsieur and Madame Dupont are dining with their guests, Monsieur Couzan and Monsieur des Barbettes.

LA BAULE: *(Sitting on the ottoman)* No matter! Let them gorge! I shall never be hungry again!

ERNESTINE: You've eaten already?

LA BAULE: I have never been hungry since the day they stole Paulette away from me.

ERNESTINE: You never eat?

LA BAULE: Only what I need to keep alive—five meals a day, but I have no appetite. *(Growing tender, he turns to* ERNESTINE.*)* Ernestine! Ah, Ernestine! They treated me very shabbily!

ERNESTINE: But Mademoiselle Paulette didn't love you.

LA BAULE: She would have learned to love me... People have to learn to love me... *(He pulls out a handkerchief.)*

ERNESTINE: Oh dear, are you going to start crying again?

LA BAULE: I can't help it. I cry all day long. I even cry in my sleep, my dreams are all wet ones...

ERNESTINE: *(Compassionately)* Does it hurt?

LA BAULE: No. It's turned into a sort of hobby. I cry for fun.

ERNESTINE: Poor young man!

LA BAULE: *(Seeing the dining room doors open)* Ah! they've finished feeding their faces!

(ERNESTINE *exits U C. The* DUPONTS *and* COUZAN *enter D L.)*

MME DUPONT: Ah, there's La Baule! Good evening, La Baule! *(She crosses in front of him to the table to pour coffee.)*

LA BAULE: Good evening, Madame Dupont... Monsieur Dupont.

DUPONT: *(Shaking his hand)* Good old La Baule. *(Introducing:)* Monsieur La Baule! My old friend Couzan!

COUZAN: Delighted, Monsieur!...

LA BAULE: Likewise, I'm sure.

DUPONT: He's the erstwhile fiancé of Madame de Trivelin.

LA BAULE: Oh, for pity's sake... Call her Paulette, not Madame de Trivelin. *(He weeps.)* Not De Trivelin!

MME DUPONT: *(To her husband)* Benjamin! Don't make him cry.

LA BAULE: When do they get back from their honeymoon?

MME DUPONT: This very night.

# ACT ONE

DUPONT: You'll be able to see them!

LA BAULE: *(Weeping)* Oh dear, oh dear, oh dear!

DUPONT: Oh no! You've cried enough for one night!

MME DUPONT: *(Handing cups of coffee to* DUPONT *and* COUZAN, *who is sitting in the easy chair.)* If it has that effect on you, it makes more sense for you to go.

LA BAULE: To think that you preferred a Trivelin to me.

DUPONT: Now look, my boy, he had everything you hadn't.

LA BAULE: Such as what? What don't I have? I'm as rich as he is.

DUPONT: That's not the point!

MME DUPONT: De Trivelin is one of the oldest names in France.

DUPONT: There were De Trivelins in the Crusades!

LA BAULE: There were La Baules there too. The only difference is they were privates!

DUPONT: My dear boy, you don't have a title!

LA BAULE: You reproach me for that, you, a republican magistrate, the son of a republican, the grandson of a republican?

DUPONT: Oh! Don't exaggerate!

LA BAULE: Your grandfather was killed on the barricades in the Revolution of '48.

DUPONT: By accident.

COUZAN: He'd gone out to buy the evening paper.

MME DUPONT: *(Who has crossed behind the table)* And besides, it's nice to have an aristocrat for a son-in-law.

LA BAULE: *(Sitting in the chair next to the table)* Which is the same as saying you'd rather have a playboy, a Don Juan!

MME DUPONT: Exactly. Monsieur de Trivelin played the field in the past. It was a guarantee of his blue blood!

LA BAULE: It's a guarantee that he'll do it again!

MME DUPONT: Certainly not. He's sown his wild oats. He'll make an excellent father...we intend to have two grandsons.

DUPONT: *(Sitting on the ottoman)* One will be a viscount, the other a chevalier.

LA BAULE: Save something for a third. What'll a third one be?

MME DUPONT: A bishop.

LA BAULE: I could have given you bishops myself.

MME DUPONT: *(To* LA BAULE*)* Would you like a cup of coffee?

LA BAULE: *(Rising)* No thank you, you barbarous parents. It's not your coffee I want, it's your daughter.

DUPONT: *(Rising)* Too late!

LA BAULE: Never mind. I'm still Paulette's fiancé.

MME DUPONT: That doesn't commit us to anything.

LA BAULE: Mark my words! You married her to a man who will make her very unhappy.

DUPONT: I certainly hope not!

LA BAULE: *(Crying)* She'll get a divorce. I feel it in my bones!

DUPONT: Oh, please, turn off the faucet!

LA BAULE: *(Rising)* You'll be in the market for another son-in-law. Swear to me that I'll be first in line...swear it.

MME DUPONT: *(Rising)* If it'll make you happy... *(To her husband)* Don't contradict him, he'll drench the carpet.

# ACT ONE

DUPONT: *(Rising)* All right. You'll be first in line. There.

LA BAULE: Thank you! I shall be your son-in-law, I'm sure of it. I'm going... I'll be back to see Paulette...and meet her detestable husband.

DUPONT: You'd better not.

LA BAULE: Yes, I will. I haven't had a good enough cry today, I haven't shed my full quota of tears. See you soon. *(He exits U C.)*

MME DUPONT: *(Going to* COUZAN *who has risen)* Well! What did you think of that young man?

COUZAN: La Bawl indeed, Madame, and the wettest of wet blankets!

DUPONT: *(Who has moved R)* His Reverence will be named Augustus.

COUZAN: Whose Reverence?

DUPONT: Our youngest...the bishop!

COUZAN: Ah! Your grandsons-to-be!

DUPONT: Yes, the viscount will be named Montmorency.

MME DUPONT: And the chevalier, Maurice!

ERNESTINE: *(Entering U C)* Monsieur, there's a gentleman outside who wants to see you!

DUPONT: A visitor at this hour! Did the gentleman give you his name?

ERNESTINE: When I asked, he said, "What for? Monsieur Dupont doesn't know me". He seems to be in a hurry...

DUPONT: Probably some lawyer who wants to get me on his side.

COUZAN: Maybe it concerns that case in Vincennes, the sex fiend who's been on the rampage.

MME DUPONT: A sex fiend? Oh, how horrible!

COUZAN: The papers have been full of nothing else for the last two days.

DUPONT: *(To* ERNESTINE*)* Well, show him in. *(To* COUZAN *and* MME DUPONT*)* We shall see!

MME DUPONT: *(To* COUZAN*)* I want to show you the room I set aside for Paulette and her husband.

COUZAN: Will they be living here?

MME DUPONT: Only until my son-in-law has purchased a townhouse.

(COUZAN *and* MME DUPONT *leave D R while* ERNESTINE *shows in* FRONTIGNAC *U C.)*

DUPONT: *(Alone, crossing L)* I'll send him about his business in two shakes.

FRONTIGNAC: *(Enters, holding a soft wide-brimmed, sombrero-like hat; he crosses D R.)* Monsieur, I'm the stranger who was just announced.

DUPONT: Please take a seat, monsieur!

FRONTIGNAC: I haven't got the time. Is your name really Dupont?

DUPONT: In the flesh… But do sit down.

FRONTIGNAC: No time… Apparently you're married?

DUPONT: *(Offended)* Dear me, I hope it isn't all that apparent?

FRONTIGNAC: Good. Call in your wife!

DUPONT: What's that?

FRONTIGNAC: I said, call in your wife.

DUPONT: Indeed? What for?

FRONTIGNAC: None of your business. *(Noticing the bell-buzzer)* Ah! A bell! *(He goes to the door in the side wall and rings.)*

# ACT ONE

DUPONT: Pardon me, but I should like an explanation.

FRONTIGNAC: *(Returning C)* No time.

DUPONT: But, monsieur...

FRONTIGNAC: No time, I tell you. *(To* ERNESTINE *who enters R)* Send for your mistress and make it snappy.

(ERNESTINE *exits D R.)*

DUPONT: Monsieur!

FRONTIGNAC: Ssh! None of your lip.

DUPONT: *(Dumbfounded)* This is incredible! Incredible!

MME DUPONT: *(Entering D R)* Did you call me, my love?

FRONTIGNAC: *(Bowing)* Madame... *(To* DUPONT*)* Is this your wife?

DUPONT: Yes, monsieur.

FRONTIGNAC: You haven't got any others?

MME DUPONT: I certainly hope not.

FRONTIGNAC: All right then. A very good night to you. *(He starts to leave.)*

DUPONT: What, he's leaving! Monsieur, monsieur!

FRONTIGNAC: *(Turning around)* Now what?

DUPONT: You're walking out, just like that?

FRONTIGNAC: I've got no further business here.

DUPONT: Excuse me, you upset my household, you disturb Madame Dupont, and then you run off without so much as leaving your name?

FRONTIGNAC: My name is Frontignac.

DUPONT: That's not good enough, monsieur!

FRONTIGNAC: *(Coming D between* DUPONT *and his wife)* Very well! If you want the story of my life! ...Let's see.

*(Looking at his watch.)* It's nine-thirty, we have until midnight.

DUPONT & MME DUPONT: *(Yelling)* Midnight!

FRONTIGNAC: Unless you want me to condense it?

*(He sits in the chair next to the table, while* MME DUPONT *sits on the sofa and* DUPONT *on the ottoman.)*

DUPONT: Condense it, condense it!

FRONTIGNAC: *(Pouring himself some coffee)* Fine! In that case, I shall skip my early years, my early travels, my early loves, my early disappointments.

MME DUPONT: Skip, skip!

FRONTIGNAC: And I shall proceed directly to the reason for my trip to Paris.

DUPONT: You live in the country?

FRONTIGNAC: *(Putting five or six lumps of sugar in his cup)* Algeria! I breed camels in Biskra.

DUPONT: *(Furious)* That's why you wanted to see my wife?

FRONTIGNAC: Where's the connection? Besides, your wife wouldn't bring a penny in those parts!

MME DUPONT: *(Put out)* Thank you!

FRONTIGNAC: *(Continuing to sugar his coffee)* You're welcome…I was a happy man…

DUPONT: *(Sarcastic)* If there isn't enough sugar, say so and I'll ring for some more.

FRONTIGNAC: No, no, don't bother, I seldom take it…I'm a wee bit diabetic… *(He drinks.)* To proceed…I was a happy man, when, five years ago, business called me to Algiers, and there I met her. She was as beautiful as a bird of paradise. I offered her my finest camel. She preferred my hand…I bestowed it and nine months later…

# ACT ONE

MME DUPONT: You were a father?

FRONTIGNAC: No, madame, I was a cuckold! The bird of paradise was nothing but a soiled dove!

DUPONT: *(Under his breath)* Nicely put!

FRONTIGNAC: One day, when I was away with a camel caravan, the hussy ran off with a Parisian she had probably met in the Biskra casino. His name was Dupont. *(He drinks.)*

MME DUPONT: Eh?

DUPONT: Keep calm, Adélaïde, it wasn't me. *(To FRONTIGNAC)* Go on.

FRONTIGNAC: *(Pours out and drinks two glasses of cognac)* Anyone else would have wept, raved, etc. Pfft! A week later I'd stopped thinking about her. Besides, my business was growing by leaps and bounds. Camels are priceless. Why, if you were to order five hundred camels for Madame Dupont's birthday, I'd be hard put to fill the order.

DUPONT: I'm not ordering anything from you.

FRONTIGNAC: It's a for-instance. *(He downs a third glass of cognac.)*

MME DUPONT: *(Sarcastic)* If you don't care for cognac, perhaps I can offer you something else.

FRONTIGNAC: No thanks, I never touch alcohol.

DUPONT: *(Aside)* Lucky for us.

FRONTIGNAC: In short, I never would have bothered about Madame Frontignac, if I hadn't just met an incomparable woman in Oran. The face of an angel, the neck of a swan, the figure of a gazelle, a wasp waist. I offered her my finest camel, she preferred my hand.

MME DUPONT: Again!

DUPONT: *(Under his breath)* I would have taken the camel.

FRONTIGNAC: What's that?

DUPONT: Nothing, nothing. Go on! This is thrilling. She preferred your hand…

FRONTIGNAC: Yes, but I can't bestow it on her until I get a divorce.

DUPONT: *(Rising)* Ah, now I understand. You're making the rounds of all the Duponts in Paris in an attempt to find your wife.

FRONTIGNAC: *(Rising when* MME DUPONT *does so)* And nab her with her lover. I've seen twenty so far. It's awful the number of Duponts there are in Paris. And not one of them has an elevator.

MME DUPONT: Believe me, monsieur, if we had known you were coming…

FRONTIGNAC: Too kind. *(To* DUPONT, *bitterly)* If my wife had had any consideration, she would have picked a lover whose name wasn't so common.

DUPONT: Thanks. *(Sarcastic)* All we can do is wish you happy hunting.

FRONTIGNAC: Oh, I'll find her! I don't suppose you have a brother or a nephew?

DUPONT: Awfully sorry. I'm the only male in my family.

FRONTIGNAC: Some family! Anyway. *(Bows)* Madame! Monsieur! *(Starts to leave)* Ah! I almost forgot. *(Giving him a card from his pocket)* Let me give you my card.

DUPONT: But…

FRONTIGNAC: No, no, don't bother seeing me out, I know the way. *(He exits quickly U C.)*

MME DUPONT: What does it say?

# ACT ONE

DUPONT: *(Reading)* Retail sales, camels starting at five hundred francs. *(Tearing up the card)* What a character!

MME DUPONT: What gall!

COUZAN: *(Entering)* May I come in?

DUPONT: Of course.

COUZAN: Well, was it about the Vincennes sex fiend?

DUPONT: No, it was some crank who wanted to divorce a dove so he could marry a gazelle with a swan's neck and a camel's waist.

COUZAN: Huh?

DUPONT: *(To ERNESTINE, who has entered R to remove the coffee and liqueurs)* Ah, Ernestine…have they delivered my painting yet?

ERNESTINE: No, monsieur. *(She exits during the next lines.)*

MME DUPONT: A painting. You bought a painting?

DUPONT: Yes, a marvelous bargain and a good deed as well…

COUZAN: And who's the painting by?

DUPONT: Zézé.

MME DUPONT: Zézé?

COUZAN: The painter's a woman?

DUPONT: Yes, a very, very old woman, a poor handicapped creature who has to earn her own living. She's an amputee at the shoulders.

*(ERNESTINE is out by now.)*

MME DUPONT: An amputee? Then how does she paint?

DUPONT: With her feet.

MME DUPONT: And how much did you pay for this smear?

DUPONT: A mere pittance. Fifteen francs, frame included.

MME DUPONT: That's not so bad after all!

DUPONT: You'll see. It's quite good. I'll put it in the billiard room.

MME DUPONT: *(Shrieking)* The billiard room! Oh my goodness!

DUPONT: What's come over you?

MME DUPONT: Lise and her fiancé have been alone in there for fifteen minutes. I've got to take a look.

DUPONT: All right, go on, my dear!

(MME DUPONT *exits L.*)

COUZAN: Benjamin Dupont!

DUPONT: Philippe Couzan?

COUZAN: Look me straight in the eye!

DUPONT: *(Embarrassed)* Why...

COUZAN: Zézé is not an old woman, Zézé is not an amputee. Zézé is a delectable blonde of twenty-eight.

DUPONT: *(Alarmed)* Be quiet, you fool!

COUZAN: You, Benjamin Dupont, judge of the Ninth District Court, are Zézé's lover?

DUPONT: For a month now. I met her at the Exhibition of Female Painters. Ah, my friend, such talent! And unselfish as all great artists are.

COUZAN: Are you going to tell me she loves you for yourself alone?

DUPONT: I am.

COUZAN: Ha ha.

# ACT ONE

DUPONT: Sneer if you like, I don't care. Just yesterday she was saying to me, I love you, I love you because you look like a Rembrandt.

COUZAN: No?

DUPONT: Yes, old friend, it turns out I look like a Rembrandt—especially from behind! So that's why she calls me Rembrandt.

(DUPONT *sits on the sofa.* COUZAN *sits on his L.*)

COUZAN: And she doesn't ask for a penny?

DUPONT: *(Hurt)* She's an artist, not a tart! "Money will never be mentioned by either of us," she declared. "Every month you'll buy a painting from me and that's all." So I bought one.

COUZAN: And she sold it to you for fifteen francs, frame and all?

DUPONT: Fifteen francs? You must be joking! Four thousand!

COUZAN: Ah! I thought so.

DUPONT: Her usual price is five thousand, but she let me have it for four, because I look like a Rembrandt.

COUZAN: You drive a hard bargain. But, you idiot, won't your wife start wondering why you've joined the painting-of-the-month club?

DUPONT: I'll tell her I'm cornering the market in Zézés.

COUZAN: You'll wind up a patron of the arts yet.

DUPONT: *(Rising and crossing L)* Well, why not, I've always wanted to be patronizing to somebody.

COUZAN: *(Rising)* Charming! Listen, Dupont, I'm not going to read you a sermon, but in your situation…as a judge…

DUPONT: So what? I can cheat on my wife as soberly as a judge.

COUZAN: Well, if that's what you want, I hope it makes you happy.

DUPONT: Seventh heaven seems like the ground floor.

COUZAN: Until the day you learn Zézé's been cheating on you.

DUPONT: *(Indignant)* Cheat on me, her?

COUZAN: Look, I don't want to sound like a killjoy, but you're no Romeo.

DUPONT: *(Annoyed)* Maybe not, but I am a Rembrandt, from behind…

COUZAN: Tails…but when it comes to heads, take a good look at yourself in the mirror.

DUPONT: Oh, stop pestering me! Watch out, my wife!

(DUPONT *crosses R.* MME DUPONT *appears in the door L.*)

MME DUPONT: *(Talking into the wings)* Stay there, but behave yourselves! *(To* DUPONT*)* What time is it, Benjamin?

DUPONT: Nearly ten, my love.

COUZAN: The newlyweds should be here any minute.

MME DUPONT: *(Coming D between* COUZAN *and* DUPONT*)* Ah, I'm so eager to see my daughter and find out how things went.

DUPONT: Aren't you ashamed to be so nosey at your age?

MME DUPONT: I'm not nosey. Poor child, she was barely out of convent school… she was so innocent.

DUPONT: True enough.

COUZAN: But what with the novels they read nowadays.

MME DUPONT: My dear Couzan, I never let my daughter read anything but fairy tales and even then

# ACT ONE

I expurgated them. And on her wedding day, she left before I could tell her what it's all about.

DUPONT: I should hope so. That's what her husband's for!

COUZAN: My dear lady, people don't do such things any more!

MME DUPONT: They did them in my day.

DUPONT: What, your mother told you what it's all about?

MME DUPONT: Certainly…and it was lucky for you she did. Otherwise I would never have let you get away with all the stunts you pulled.

LISE: *(Entering quickly L followed by* GONTRAN*)* Mama, they're here, the carriage just stopped at the door.

MME DUPONT: *(About to faint)* She's here, my child, my little girl!

DUPONT: The count and countess!

MME DUPONT: Oh, my gracious! My nerves… I'm so happy! *(She falters and drops onto the chair next to the table.)*

COUZAN: *(Hurrying forward)* Come, come, dear lady.

DUPONT: Adélaïde, be a man for five minutes.

MME DUPONT: I shall.

*(She rises. The door U C opens and* PAULETTE *appears, followed by* DE TRIVELIN. *Travelling clothes, overnight bags.)*

PAULETTE: *(Throwing herself in her mother's arms)* Oh! Mama! Mama!

MME DUPONT: Paulette!

DUPONT: Son-in-law!

DE TRIVELIN: *(Shaking his hand)* My dear Monsieur Dupont!

DUPONT: Monsieur Dupont! You ought to call me father-in-law.

DE TRIVELIN: My dear father-in-law. *(To LISE)* Hello, Lise dear!

LISE: Welcome back, Robert!

DE TRIVELIN: Ah! and Des Barbettes...Monsieur Couzan.

*(Handshakes.* MME DUPONT *is R with* PAULETTE.*)*

DUPONT: *(To his wife who is still kissing* PAULETTE*)* Say, Adélaïde, I've got dibs on the Countess after you. Leave some for others.

PAULETTE: Ah, papa! Dear papa!

*(She throws herself into* DUPONT*'s arms.)*

MME DUPONT: *(To* DE TRIVELIN, *opening her arms)* Well, Robert, now it's your turn. What are you waiting for?

DE TRIVELIN: An empty space, mama-in-law! *(He kisses her.)*

PAULETTE: *(To* LISE, *kissing her)* Hello, Lisette! *(Seeing* GONTRAN *and* COUZAN*)* Gontran! ...And my godfather! What a nice surprise!

MME DUPONT: She's radiant, isn't she, Couzan?

COUZAN: Radiant!

PAULETTE: I never felt better in my life.

MME DUPONT: *(Roguishly, giving* DE TRIVELIN *a little tap)* As for Robert, he looks a little worn out to me.

DE TRIVELIN: Think so?

DUPONT: That's a fact!

PAULETTE: *(Naively)* But I should be just as tired as he is.

# ACT ONE

DUPONT: *(Merrily)* Objection sustained!

MME DUPONT: Now tell me— *(Stopping short)* Lise, go into a corner with Monsieur des Barbettes. *(Continuing)* Tell me, children, is there anything on the way?

PAULETTE: Yes!

COUZAN, DUPONT, & MME DUPONT: *(Quickly)* Ah!

(COUZAN, DUPONT, PAULETTE, MME DUPONT *and* DE TRIVELIN *in a row.* LISE *and* GONTRAN *U L.)*

PAULETTE: We bought gifts in Venice, and they should be arriving any day now.

MME DUPONT: That's not what I meant. *(Whispers to* DE TRIVELIN *while* LISE *joins her sister)* How is Montmorency coming along?

DE TRIVELIN: Montmorency?

MME DUPONT: The viscount!

DE TRIVELIN: What viscount?

DUPONT: My grandson, of course!

DE TRIVELIN: *(Very embarrassed)* He's quite well, thank you...still a bit vague.

MME DUPONT: *(Ribaldly)* You're right, of course...it would make more sense to create him here in Paris.

DUPONT: *(Laughing)* In comfort—with your feet up.

MME DUPONT: Come along, Paulette, I'll show you your room.

PAULETTE: Yes, mama.

DE TRIVELIN: I'll come with you.

MME DUPONT: No, no, we'll be back in a minute... Stay with the gentlemen...I have to have a chinwag with my daughter.

DE TRIVELIN: *(Anxiously)* What about?

MME DUPONT: *(Whisper)* I want to find out if you've made her happy.

DE TRIVELIN: *(Aside)* Dammit!

MME DUPONT: Coming, Paulette?

PAULETTE: Right away, mama, I'm getting my overnight bag.

*(She exits D R with MME DUPONT.)*

LISE: *(Whisper to GONTRAN)* Nobody's paying attention to us, let's go in the dining room.

GONTRAN: Great!

*(They disappear U L.)*

DE TRIVELIN: *(Standing near the door D R, very upset)* Dammit, dammit! dammit!

DUPONT: What's the matter, son-in-law? Is there something on your mind? You look upset!

COUZAN: Indeed you do!

DE TRIVELIN: If you only knew!

DUPONT: What? Do you have any complaints to make about Paulette?

DE TRIVELIN: Complaints? Why, Paulette is exquisite. Paulette is an angel!

DUPONT: Aren't you satisfied with your welcome home?

DE TRIVELIN: *(Protesting)* Of course I am!

DUPONT: Your mother-in-law is crazy about you.

COUZAN: Which is most unusual, considering how that species has it in for all mankind!

DE TRIVELIN: She's crazy about me...at the moment. But in a few seconds, she'll come bursting out of that room, wild with rage, her eyes bulging out of her

# ACT ONE 21

head…and insult me! The things I'll have to put up with, God! What I'll have to go through!

DUPONT: What do you mean?

COUZAN: Am I in the way?

DE TRIVELIN: No, no, no, my dear Couzan, as a godfather you have a right to be here.

DUPONT: Well, speak out, son-in-law, speak out!

DE TRIVELIN: Just a moment. Madame Dupont will be back any minute and I'd prefer to make my explanation once and for all.

*(A furious MME DUPONT appears D R.)*

MME DUPONT: *(Barely in control of herself)* Count Robert de Trivelin!

DE TRIVELIN: *(To DUPONT and COUZAN)* Here it comes!

MME DUPONT: You are a miserable excuse for a man!

DUPONT: What's the matter, what is it?

DE TRIVELIN: Please, hear me out before you reach your verdict!

*(DE TRIVELIN gestures to them to sit down. MME DUPONT sits on the sofa, DUPONT on the ottoman, and COUZAN in the easy chair. DE TRIVELIN stands between DUPONT and the table.)*

DE TRIVELIN: When I asked for Paulette's hand, I adored her, I still adore her, you needn't worry about that. I was a playboy… And you demanded an engagement period of six months.

DUPONT: That's right! You can't complain, you saw your fiancé every day.

DE TRIVELIN: And can you imagine what those six months were like for a man head over heels in love, a faithful lover and consequently a love-starved lover, always being told: Look but don't touch. *(To MME

DUPONT.) You'll probably say, "You should have satisfied your hunger in any convenient restaurant".

MME DUPONT: Certainly not. I wouldn't have said anything of the kind!

DE TRIVELIN: I loved Paulette too much to cheat on her! I am proud to declare, I might perhaps cheat on my wife, but I have never cheated on my fiancée. So, the condition I was in those last few days...

COUZAN: A bridegroom's usual condition.

DUPONT: *(Merrily)* I was that way myself! *(To* MME DUPONT*)* Remember?

MME DUPONT: Don't interrupt.

DE TRIVELIN: The wedding day arrived! What a day! Ceremony at the church, wedding breakfast, shaking people's hands as mechanically as flipping pancakes! Finally, at ten o'clock, Paulette and I made our escape... Ah! what a relief! No more obligations, no more relatives...

MME DUPONT: Thank you very much!

DE TRIVELIN: When our train pulled out, I clasped my little Paulette in my arms. She was trembling...I started talking all sorts of stuff and nonsense, but delicious nonsense...

DUPONT: Yes, so did I with my wife. *(To* MME DUPONT*)* Remember?

MME DUPONT: *(To* DE TRIVELIN*)* Go on!

DE TRIVELIN: Gradually, she became more confident... our talk was sweet, then tender, then tenderer, then impassioned...I had resolved, however, to wait till we got to Brussels before I became my wife's husband... But little by little I felt a new resolve stiffening within me, not to wait till Belgium, but to pluck the hymeneal blossom on the sacred soil of our fatherland!

# ACT ONE

DUPONT: Bravo!

DE TRIVELIN: I was beside myself. She was breathless with an emotion she had never known before... Oblivious to the outside world, we hadn't noticed that the train was slowing down and just at the moment when the loveliest of my dreams was about to be consummated... the door opened and in stepped a man in uniform, shouting, Anything to declare? It was Customs! *(He falls onto a chair.)*

DUPONT: *(Laughing)* Ah, that must have been annoying!

DE TRIVELIN: Don't laugh! The shock was brutal. I threw the intrusive bureaucrat out of the compartment. But the spell was broken! I must have suffered some kind of nervous prostration. Because, when the train pulled out again...I had nothing to declare!

COUZAN: Oh dear, oh dear.

DUPONT: Come, come...that's impossible!

DE TRIVELIN: It's the truth... While I was struggling to pull myself together, Paulette fell asleep, without the slightest idea of what had happened...I respected her slumber...and in Brussels she finished out the night as serenely as she had begun it.

DUPONT: But the next day?

DE TRIVELIN: The next day, I don't know how, but at the moment of truth, the image of that customs inspector popped into my mind...and...I was shot to hell!

DUPONT: Stop thinking about customs inspectors!

DE TRIVELIN: Believe me, I don't do it on purpose!

DUPONT: But the day after that?

DE TRIVELIN: I lost all my self-confidence... And you see, in such cases, when a man loses his self-confidence, he loses everything. *(Rising)* Germany...

Switzerland...Italy...wherever we went, that diabolical customs man was on my trail...each and every time, just at the critical moment...I could hear his snotty voice saying, "Anything to declare?" And each and every time there'd be a droop in my...spirits. *(He falls back onto the chair.)* Now you know the sorry truth.

DUPONT: And what does Paulette have to say about this?

MME DUPONT: The dear innocent child hasn't a clue. Just now, no matter what question I asked, she stared at me with big round eyes as if I was asking her the name of Cleopatra's grandmother.

DUPONT: Blast! *(To* COUZAN*)* What do you think?

COUZAN: I think if it goes on much longer, His Reverence the Bishop will be late for his ordination!

DE TRIVELIN: *(Rising)* Ah, that customs inspector! And that phrase!

MME DUPONT: *(Rising)* But, for heaven's sake, when people are that way they don't get married, they enter monasteries!

DUPONT: *(Rising)* And even then, only certain orders!

DE TRIVELIN: No sarcasm please! It's no laughing matter!

DUPONT: Nevertheless, monsieur, this situation might go on forever.

MME DUPONT: And I want grandchildren, I insist on it!

DUPONT: We insist!

DE TRIVELIN: So do I! Give me a chance to recover from this accident—it's merely a temporary setback.

MME DUPONT: *(To* DE TRIVELIN*)* You know what I think? You brought my daughter nothing but a playboy's leftovers!

# ACT ONE

DE TRIVELIN: That's a lie! A monstrous lie!

DUPONT: And even then, if you knew how to reheat leftovers!

DE TRIVELIN: *(Losing his temper)* Monsieur Dupont!

MME DUPONT: *(To* DUPONT*)* After all, this whole business is *your* fault.

DUPONT: Mine?

MME DUPONT: If Monsieur hadn't insisted on having an aristocrat for a son-in-law, a rake, a debauchee!

DUPONT: Excuse me! You were the one who wanted to see your daughter a countess.

*(They argue nose to nose in front of* DE TRIVELIN, *jostling him.)*

MME DUPONT: *(Protesting)* Me? Me?

DUPONT: Absolutely! I wouldn't hear of it…I'm a republican from way back, son and grandson of republicans, my grandfather was killed on the barricades.

MME DUPONT: I always told you: *(Pointing at* DE TRIVELIN*)* I don't trust that fellow's face.

DUPONT: Excuse me, I was the one who said that!

DE TRIVELIN: *(Separating them)* You know, I'm standing right here.

COUZAN: Now, now, my friends, calm down…and let me say something.

MME DUPONT: Mind your own business, Couzan. *(To* DE TRIVELIN.*)* As for you, monsieur…here's my ultimatum! I give you three days…

DE TRIVELIN: Three days? What for?

MME DUPONT: If, at the end of three days, you have not become your wife's husband, we shall sue for divorce.

DE TRIVELIN: Divorce?

DUPONT: Three days! Not another night!

MME DUPONT: And once the divorce is filed, we'll bestow her hand on La Baule.

DE TRIVELIN: La Baule? What is the world is La Baule?

DUPONT: A fine fellow who adores Paulette. We wronged him when we preferred you to him.

DE TRIVELIN: Huh?

DUPONT: Besides, we've arranged it with him...he's first in line.

DE TRIVELIN: First in what line?

(ERNESTINE *appears D R. The lineup is* COUZAN, DUPONT, MME DUPONT, *and* DE TRIVELIN.)

ERNESTINE: *(To* DE TRIVELIN*)* Monsieur.

DE TRIVELIN: *(Exasperated)* What? What is it?

ERNESTINE: Madame would like the keys.

DE TRIVELIN: The keys? What keys?

MME DUPONT: *(Sarcastic)* The keys to the trunk. Go on! Make yourself useful, since you can't make yourself enjoyable!

DE TRIVELIN: *(Indicating* ERNESTINE, *and in a whisper)* Please, don't let everyone in on this secret. *(To* ERNESTINE*)* Very well, I'll be right there!

(ERNESTINE *exits U C.)*

DE TRIVELIN: Divorce!...first in line! We'll see about that! *(He exits D R.)*

COUZAN: *(Rising)* Poor boy, it's not his fault.

MME DUPONT: Well, it's sure as hell not mine!

DUPONT: Or mine!

# ACT ONE

ERNESTINE: *(Entering U C and announcing)* Monsieur La Baule.

DUPONT: The man of the hour!

MME DUPONT: Ah, come in, son, do come in!

(LA BAULE *appears, weeping.* ERNESTINE *exits.*)

COUZAN: *(Aside)* The human waterworks!

LA BAULE: I've come to say goodbye.

DUPONT & MME DUPONT: Goodbye?

LA BAULE: Yes...I simply do not have the strength to live in Paris...I shall go south to weep: I'm leaving tomorrow morning.

MME DUPONT: No!

LA BAULE: Sorry! ...Two days from now, Monte Carlo will be inundated with my tears.

MME DUPONT: No, I tell you. You'll leave three days from now.

DUPONT: If you leave at all.

LA BAULE: Why?

MME DUPONT: Because during that time, it may happen...that nothing will happen.

*(The lineup:* COUZAN, MME DUPONT, LA BAULE, *and* DUPONT*)*

DUPONT: And in that case, you can marry Paulette.

LA BAULE: Huh? Me? Marry Paulette?

DUPONT: Yes, we're rescuing her from De Trivelin.

LA BAULE: Ah! I knew it! That villain made her unhappy.

MME DUPONT: Not exactly, but he didn't make her happy!

LA BAULE: I don't follow.

DUPONT: Listen to this!

COUZAN: But you aren't going to tell this gentleman about...

DUPONT: Butt out or I'll get annoyed...

(DUPONT *whispers in* LA BAULE's *ear.*)

LA BAULE: *(Gasping)* Oh!

MME DUPONT: And every time he sees a customs inspector, things take a downward turn!

LA BAULE: No! That's a good one! That's what those playboys are like!

DUPONT: *Play* boy? Not even a rehearsal!

MME DUPONT: And since you're first in line, if my daughter fails to become his wife in three days' time, she is yours.

LA BAULE: *(Emotionally)* Oh, Madame! I'll make her happy, I will, I'll make her happy ten times if I do it once! *(He weeps.)*

DUPONT: No, no! Stop crying!

LA BAULE: *(Throwing himself into* DUPONT's *arms)* It's joy, these are tears of joy!

MME DUPONT: Well, how about me, dear boy! Come to my arms, my son!

(LA BAULE *throws himself into* MME DUPONT's *arms, while* DE TRIVELIN *appears D R.*)

DE TRIVELIN: *(To* DUPONT*)* Who is the gentleman kissing your wife?

DUPONT: Your wife's fiancée, monsieur!

DE TRIVELIN: Beg pardon?

DUPONT: This is La Baule.

# ACT ONE

DE TRIVELIN: Indeed! *(Going to* LA BAULE*)* Monsieur, I have a sound piece of advice for you, and that is to vacate the premises at once.

LA BAULE: Excuse me, monsieur, I don't know you.

DE TRIVELIN: I am Count De Trivelin.

LA BAULE: Ah! You're the customs inspector fellow!

DE TRIVELIN: *(Beside himself)* What, they've gone and told him... *(To* LA BAULE*)* Monsieur, I declare...

LA BAULE: *(Sarcastic)* Oh, you have nothing to declare!

DUPONT & MME DUPONT: *(Laughing and applauding)* Bravo!

DE TRIVELIN: Get out! ...Get out, monsieur, before I do you an injury.

LA BAULE: *(Losing his temper)* Monsieur!

MME DUPONT: No, no, ignore him!

DUPONT: Come back in three days' time.

LA BAULE: Very well, I shall withdraw, to avoid a quarrel with this gentleman. *(To* MME DUPONT, *as he glances at* DE TRIVELIN *in defiance)* Good night, mother-in-law...

MME DUPONT: Goodnight, son-in-law.

LA BAULE: *(To* DE TRIVELIN*)* As for you, monsieur, we shall meet sooner than you think!

DE TRIVELIN: *(Furious)* Monsieur!

LA BAULE: Monsieur!

MME DUPONT: *(Dragging him away)* Come, dear boy, come away.

LA BAULE: Oh, he doesn't scare me!

(LA BAULE *exits U C, dragged by* DUPONT *and* MME DUPONT.)

DE TRIVELIN: Oh, the filthy swine! The nasty sneaking lowdown...! *(He sits in the chair L.)*

COUZAN: *(Crossing to him)* Come, come, calm down!

DE TRIVELIN: I'm a ruined man, I'm done for!

COUZAN: The hell you are! Your case is far from desperate. It's quite common, purely a psychological problem! If only your mother-in-law were a psychiatrist!

DE TRIVELIN: *(Rising)* No thanks...she's dangerous enough as it is! *(He sits in the easy chair.)*

COUZAN: *(Following him)* You're high-strung, over-sensitive, that's all. Your mishap is normal enough... Why, even I...

DE TRIVELIN: What, you too?

COUZAN: *(Sitting on the ottoman)* Quite so. My late wife, rest in peace, didn't taste marital joys for two months after the wedding.

DE TRIVELIN: Really? ...And all because of a customs inspector?

COUZAN: No, in my case it was a heifer.

DE TRIVELIN: A heifer?

COUZAN: Yes. My late wife, rest in peace, was from Normandy—in the provinces they have a custom on wedding days of playing practical jokes on the newlyweds. The guests of my late wife, rest in peace, thought it witty to hide a heifer behind a screen in the nuptial bedchamber.

DE TRIVELIN: No!

COUZAN: What a sense of humor they have in the provinces! At first I failed to notice it, but just at the moment when—you follow me...?

# ACT ONE

DE TRIVELIN: Yes, yes, the moment when my customs inspector burst into the compartment…

COUZAN: Exactly! The heifer started calling for its mother.

(DE TRIVELIN *moos.*)

COUZAN: Bull's eye! You can imagine the look on my face.

DE TRIVELIN: And on hers too!

COUZAN: I was furious and sent that underaged ruminant hurtling down the stairs a lot faster than she had come up them. Then I attempted to resume my barely initiated dialogue. Ah well…nothing doing! Nobody home!

DE TRIVELIN: Same as me!

COUZAN: The next day, nothing doing again, and the day after as well… *(Rising.)* That animal was haunting me! I could see it before my eyes, bleating for its mother! Try and pluck your orange blossoms under those conditions!

DE TRIVELIN: Good grief! Then what?

COUZAN: *(Sitting down again)* Night after night, week after week…like you, I thought: I'm ruined…washed up!

DE TRIVELIN: And then?

COUZAN: Then, in desperation, I consulted a friend of mine, a doctor…I told him I feared that I had forever lost my faculty of…communication, and he replied, "You're an idiot, put your trust in Clemency!"

DE TRIVELIN: Divine clemency?

COUZAN: No, Clemency, the local tart.

DE TRIVELIN: So you put your trust in Clemency?

COUZAN: *(Rising)* And Clemency restored my self-esteem!

DE TRIVELIN: *(Rising)* Really?

COUZAN: *(Looking skyward)* That was the only time I cheated on my late wife, rest in peace, but it was for the sake of her happiness.

DE TRIVELIN: And ever since then…no more communication gaps?

COUZAN: Never! Except…

DE TRIVELIN: *(Worried)* What?

COUZAN: Ever since then, I can't digest veal!

DUPONT: *(Entering D L followed by* GONTRAN *and* LISE*)* It's time for you to be going home, my young friend!

COUZAN: I'll walk you downstairs, Monsieur des Barbettes.

DUPONT: Lise, tell your mother and sister that these gentlemen are about to leave.

LISE: Yes, papa… *(She exits U R.)*

(COUZAN *and* DE TRIVELIN *have gone U a bit and chat in an undertone during the next lines.)*

GONTRAN: *(Referring to* LISE; *to* DUPONT*)* She's so sweet!

DUPONT: Isn't she?

GONTRAN: I intend to make her happy!

DUPONT: I expect you to.

GONTRAN: As happy as her sister! *(He goes U to* COUZAN.*)*

DUPONT: *(To himself)* Her sister, poor child… It just occurred to me!… *(Aloud)* Des Barbettes, come over here a minute… *(Quietly and affably)* You do have a mistress, don't you?

GONTRAN: *(Quickly)* I swear I don't!

## ACT ONE

DUPONT: *(Anxiously)* Ah! ...How long has this been going on?

GONTRAN: Ever since I fell in love with Mademoiselle Lise, six months ago.

DUPONT: *(Aside)* Six months, just like the other one. Could it be that he too...?

GONTRAN: *(Startled, aside)* Why is he asking all this?

DUPONT: *(In an undertone)* Des Barbettes, what's your opinion of customs inspectors?

GONTRAN: *(Dumbfounded)* Customs inspectors? They are the sworn foes of contraband.

DUPONT: *(To himself)* Contraband, indeed! *(To GONTRAN)* Be sure to come and have a talk with me tomorrow morning.

GONTRAN: Yes, Monsieur Dupont... *(Aside)* What's got into him?

COUZAN: *(Who, during these lines, has spoken in an undertone with DE TRIVELIN; aloud)* I repeat, the remedy is infallible!

MME DUPONT: *(Entering D R, followed by LISE)* My dear Couzan, Paulette asks me to excuse her, she is undressed.

COUZAN: No excuse needed. Goodnight, dear lady.

MME DUPONT: Goodnight, my dear friend. *(To GONTRAN)* Goodnight, Gontran!

GONTRAN: May I request permission to kiss my fiancée?

MME DUPONT: My young friend, you know my principles, you may not kiss your fiancée until she becomes your wife.

DUPONT: However, if you absolutely insist on kissing a person of the opposite sex, there stands your mother-in-law-to-be.

GONTRAN: With pleasure. *(He kisses her.)*

DUPONT: *(To* GONTRAN*)* Go on, don't be shy, be emphatic!

COUZAN: *(To* LISE*)* Goodnight, Lisette.

LISE: I'll see you out, dear Monsieur Couzan.

COUZAN: *(Undertone to* DE TRIVELIN, *shaking his hand)* Infallible!

DE TRIVELIN: Thanks!

LISE: *(Undertone to* GONTRAN*)* We can snatch a kiss in the hallway.

(COUZAN *and* GONTRAN *exit U C, escorted by* LISE.)

MME DUPONT: *(Who has gone U R with* DUPONT*)* And now we leave you, Count De Trivelin.

DE TRIVELIN: *(Conciliatory)* Come now, mother-in-law.

MME DUPONT: Mother-in-law indeed! We'll discuss that three days hence.

DUPONT: You know what you've got to do?

DE TRIVELIN: *(Exasperated)* Good Lord! Yes, I know!

DUPONT: Three days!

MME DUPONT: That's more than God needed to create man.

DUPONT: And woman!

DE TRIVELIN: *(Pleading)* For pity's sake!

MME DUPONT: Goodnight, Count De Trivelin.

DUPONT: Goodnight, descendant of virile crusaders!

# ACT ONE

MME DUPONT: Come along, Benjamin, let's go to bed. *(Undertone, as she modestly casts down her eyes.)* And let's set him a good example.

DUPONT: *(aside)* Huh! Ah! No!

*(They leave R.)*

DE TRIVELIN: *(Alone)* Three days! Not even a week, the notice you'd give a servant!

PAULETTE: *(Entering D R, in charming nightdress, arms and shoulders bare)* What's keeping you, Robert?

DE TRIVELIN: My wife! My dear little wife! *(Aside)* Three days! *(To* PAULETTE*)* I was just thinking of you.

PAULETTE: Ah!

DE TRIVELIN: Come sit down here... *(He takes her by the hand and seats her on the ottoman; to himself.)* Come on, show some spunk! No more customs inspectors here! Nothing stands in your way!

PAULETTE: And what were you thinking about me? Tell me...are you on bad terms with mama?

DE TRIVELIN: *(Quickly)* Not at all!

PAULETTE: *(Crosses R and sits on the sofa)* She came into my room and asked me a lot of questions.

DE TRIVELIN: *(Between his teeth)* The old bitch!

PAULETTE: What?

DE TRIVELIN: *(Sitting on the sofa)* A twitch...I've got a twitch in my neck... And what was your saintly lady mother asking you?

PAULETTE: Strange things. I couldn't understand them all. She seemed very put out with you...I thought you must have quarrelled.

DE TRIVELIN: Quite the contrary...your mother adores me...she was just now comparing me with God, so you see!

PAULETTE: I'm so glad... Are you coming to bed? *(She starts to get up.)*

DE TRIVELIN: No, not yet, dear Paulette. *(He pulls her back down.)* I'm so glad to have you right here beside me, all to myself.

PAULETTE: I was all to yourself on the honeymoon!

DE TRIVELIN: Yes, but then there were things on my mind, distractions.

PAULETTE: You were always worried we'd miss the train.

DE TRIVELIN: Exactly. Here I'm not worried I'll miss the train. *(Placing his arm round her waist)* You're mine... You're my wife, my dear little wife!

PAULETTE: I have been for a month!

DE TRIVELIN: That's not the same thing... Let's resume our conversation where we left off a month ago.

PAULETTE: On the train.

DE TRIVELIN: *(Rising quickly)* Let's stop talking about trains! Leave the train out of it!

*(PAULETTE rises.)*

DE TRIVELIN: Ah! Paulette! My Lélette! *(He takes her in his arms.)*

PAULETTE: What's come over you? You're acting so queer this evening!

DE TRIVELIN: No, I'm not acting queer, don't say queer!

*(DE TRIVELIN kisses PAULETTE frantically.)*

PAULETTE: Stop it! You're making me feel all shivery!

DE TRIVELIN: And you're making me feel all prickly!

*(DE TRIVELIN kisses PAULETTE.)*

PAULETTE: You never kissed me like that before!

# ACT ONE

DE TRIVELIN: *(Ardently)* Didn't I? Didn't I?

PAULETTE: I feel just like Little Red Riding Hood with the wolf.

DE TRIVELIN: A nice wolf, darling, who's going to eat you up.

PAULETTE: Grandmother, what big bright eyes you have!

DE TRIVELIN: The better to charm you with, my dear.

(DE TRIVELIN *kisses* PAULETTE.)

PAULETTE: Grandmother, what burning lips you have!

DE TRIVELIN: The better to kiss you with, my dear.

PAULETTE: Grandmother, what trembling hands you have!

DE TRIVELIN: The better to carry you off with, my dear!

PAULETTE: Robert! Robert!

(DE TRIVELIN *draws her into the next room, turning off the light-switch near the door. Blackout. The stage is empty. Then we hear the entry door open.* LA BAULE *appears in the uniform of a customs inspector. He wears a false beard and holds a lighted candle.*)

LA BAULE: *(Comes D C, lifts his false beard)* It's me! *(He puts the beard back in place.)* Five hundred francs to a customs man at the Gare du Nord to lend me his uniform, two hundred francs to Ernestine for the key to the apartment, and here I am... Oh no, you won't be my Paulette's husband! Let's see! Their bedroom is over there... *(He starts towards the door R and looks through the keyhole.)* Oh my God! Not a minute too soon! *(He opens the door.)*

DE TRIVELIN'S VOICE: *(Crying out)* Ah!

LA BAULE: *(Loudly)* Anything to declare?

DE TRIVELIN'S VOICE: *(As before)* Ah!

(LA BAULE *closes the door, blows out the candle, and runs out U C. Blackout.*)

DE TRIVELIN: *(Enters in shirtsleeves)* Where is he? Where is he? *(He quickly switches on the lights, opens the door U C.)* Nobody! Nobody! *(With absurd rage)* Oh great! Now I'm having hallucinations!

PAULETTE: *(Offstage)* Robert, are you coming?

DE TRIVELIN: Never mind, never mind, go to sleep. *(Aside)* Only two days left! *(He sinks onto the ottoman.)*

### END ACT ONE

# ACT TWO

(*A painter's studio. Luxurious furnishings, in somewhat whorish taste. Main entrance door U R, on a side wall. Two doors L. U C, a large studio window. Small practicable window, only one side of which opens, U L on a side wall. Near the U entry, a small screen. D L of the big window, a table; on it, a Roman warrior's helmet. Between this table and the screen, an easel holding a painting of the legendary founders of Rome, the twins Romulus and Remus. A red toga is hanging over one edge of the easel. L, a chaise longue. R of the chaise, a huge easel set a bit on an angle. Small painting on the easel and, leaning against the back of it, a huge canvas depicting a life-sized, scantily clad woman. A Roman warrior's spear is also leaning against it. A stool between the easel and the chaise longue. R, a third easel, with a painting on which* GOLD MEDAL *is working, seated on a stool, at the rise of the curtain. Chair L of this easel and stool R of it, with an open paintbox on it. D L of the chairs, a sort of platform to be mounted by the model. R of the entrance doors a small cabinet. Between the two doors L, a secretary. Plenty of canvases on the wall, knickknacks, furniture, etc*)

(*Important note: The costumes of* DUPONT, DE TRIVELIN, *and* FRONTIGNAC *in this act must be, if not absolutely identical, at least similar in color, so that, at first sight, they might be confused.*)

(*As the curtain rises,* ZÉZÉ *is seated on the chaise longue.* MARIETTE, *sitting on a low chair, is giving her a manicure.*)

*On the stool near the chaise longue, nail polish, a small brush, etc.* GOLD MEDAL *is working R.)*

ZÉZÉ: Will you be done soon, Mariette?

MARIETTE: Right away, madame.

ZÉZÉ: Say, did you see the papers this morning?

MARIETTE: The picture post, as usual.

ZÉZÉ: Anything new?

MARIETTE: No, nothing important. A massacre here, an earthquake there.

ZÉZÉ: What about the Vincennes case? ...That sex fiend. Have they caught him yet?

MARIETTE: I doubt it. They'll never catch him. He's too sharp!

GOLD MEDAL: *(Working away)* They haven't even got a good description. At least not of his face.

MARIETTE: *(Rising)* Now you're done, madame.

ZÉZÉ: *(Rising)* At last! It's two o'clock and I'm barely ready.

MARIETTE: Oh, Monsieur Rembrandt never comes before two-thirty.

*(During the next lines,* MARIETTE *locks the nail polish, brush, etc, in the secretary, replaces the chair next to the desk, and puts the stool at the end of the chaise longue next to the easel.)*

ZÉZÉ: Soon enough. What a crashing bore!

GOLD MEDAL: Maybe so, but I find the old magistrate simpatico.

ZÉZÉ: *(Crossing R)* You don't know him the way I do!

GOLD MEDAL: But I know him through you... You told me he's mad about my painting.

# ACT TWO

ZÉZÉ: True. Many's the time he's said, Zézé, your hands are worth a fortune.

GOLD MEDAL: Hmm! If only he knew you've never held a paint brush in your life and the work's all done by a one-time winner of the Academy gold medal.

ZÉZÉ: *(Sitting L of the easel, next to* GOLD MEDAL*)* He fell for it hook, line and sinker.

GOLD MEDAL: Like all the rest...

ZÉZÉ: *(Stretching)* That was a wonderful idea of mine, wasn't it! If it weren't for this cover, I'd have no position in society at all. Not after leaving my husband. I would have been Zézé the tramp, pure and simple. Now that I'm an artist, I get mentioned in the papers, exhibited at the Salon, I'm unrivalled.

GOLD MEDAL: And to think that when I used to sign my pictures with my own name, I was never offered fifty francs, even if I threw in the frame!

ZÉZÉ: *(Rising)* Because you don't give bonuses. I do! *(Placing her right foot on the little stool and stretching.)* I don't know what's the matter with me today. My nerves are on edge.

GOLD MEDAL: It's the first day of spring.

ZÉZÉ: Spring? You're right. That's why I've got ants in my pants!

GOLD MEDAL: Rembrandt will be here soon, and you can celebrate springtime with him!

ZÉZÉ: Celebrate springtime with him! Oh no! You can't mean it! I don't know who I will celebrate springtime with, but I'm positive...

GOLD MEDAL: That Rembrandt will be hoodwinked once again!

ZÉZÉ: Today, Gold Medal, I need love, no matter how short the supply is. So, as soon as Rembrandt gets here, I'll give him the bum's rush for the day. *(The doorbell rings offstage.)* Right on cue! There he is... *(To* MARIETTE.*)* Show him in.

*(To* GOLD MEDAL, *who has risen)*

ZÉZÉ: And as for you, quick! ...Hand me those brushes and palette.

GOLD MEDAL: Should I hang out in the kitchen?

ZÉZÉ: No, put on the toga and the helmet.

GOLD MEDAL: Right. *(He puts on the toga and the helmet, then climbs on to the little stool, after grabbing the spear leaning against the easel C.)*

ZÉZÉ: Wait and see how efficiently I'll adjourn this session of court. *(She sits down before the easel R.)*

GOLD MEDAL: What story will you palm off on him? *(He takes a pose facing the audience, left hand upraised, spear in his right hand.)*

ZÉZÉ: With dopes like him, you can take your pick!

GOLD MEDAL: *(To the audience)* And to think I had a fellowship from the National Endowment for the Arts!

MARIETTE: *(Entering U and announcing)* Monsieur Rembrandt!

DUPONT: *(Entering with a bouquet of lilies of the valley)* Good afternoon, Zézé, my love!

ZÉZÉ: *(Pretending to paint)* Good afternoon, Rembrandt! *(Noticing the bouquet)* Oh! Lilies of the valley!

DUPONT: *(Gallantly)* The flower of springtime! *(Singing while he puts the bouquet in a vase on the cabinet.)* The flowers that bloom in the spring, tra la. *(Coming D between* GOLD MEDAL *and* ZÉZÉ*)* At work already?

ZÉZÉ: Since daybreak...I'm putting the finishing touches on this canvas.

# ACT TWO

DUPONT: Allow me to kiss the finishing touch of this hand, the hand of both an unrivalled master and an adorable mistress.

GOLD MEDAL: *(Aside)* The melon-head's a bit overripe!

DUPONT: *(Admiring the painting)* Admirable! Really admirable!

GOLD MEDAL: *(Aside)* But the melon-head has got taste.

DUPONT: Ah, Zézé, Zézé! *(He leans over to kiss her.)*

ZÉZÉ: *(Indicating the palette)* Careful!

DUPONT: *(Laughing)* That's right. Hands off, wet paint.

*(DUPONT turns around and hangs his hat on GOLD MEDAL's left hand. GOLD MEDAL takes the hat with his right hand. DUPONT observes this in bewilderment.)*

DUPONT: Goodness! He's alive! He's human!

ZÉZÉ: Yes, he's an old Italian! Signor Pastafazool. Don't worry about him, he doesn't know a word of our language.

DUPONT: Ugly brute, isn't he? He ought to pose for the gargoyles on Notre-Dame. *(He walks up and puts his hat on the easel where ZÉZÉ is sitting, then crosses R.)*

ZÉZÉ: *(In a whisper, leaning toward GOLD MEDAL)* Poor Gold Medal!

GOLD MEDAL: *(In an undertone)* He gets on my nerves.

DUPONT: Zézé, my love, get rid of that freak. I'm longing to be alone with you.

ZÉZÉ: Is that so! *(Aside)* Not if I can help it! *(She rises and pretends to be dizzy.)* Oh!

DUPONT: What's the matter?

ZÉZÉ: A touch of giddiness.

DUPONT: *(Worried)* Giddiness? Come and sit down.

*(He leads her to the chaise longue and sits L of her.)*

ZÉZÉ: I've been having dizzy spells for several days now.

DUPONT: Really!

ZÉZÉ: And I've had cravings.

DUPONT: *(Moved)* Bless my soul! Can it be that you… that we…?

ZÉZÉ: *(Throwing herself in his arms)* I think so, my dear.

DUPONT: *(Rising, ecstatic)* A little Zézé! I've created a little Zézé…

GOLD MEDAL: *(Aside, watching DUPONT)* Get a load of him!

DUPONT: *(To GOLD MEDAL)* And that idiot Trivelin isn't even capable of…

GOLD MEDAL: *(In an Italian accent)* Ch'è cosa?

DUPONT: Nothing.

*(To ZÉZÉ who has risen and whom he forces back into her seat.)*

DUPONT: Don't lift a finger, sit down…tell me…what sort of cravings do you have? *(He sits beside her.)*

ZÉZÉ: Irresistible ones.

DUPONT: They have to be satisfied right away, or else the baby will have a birthmark.

ZÉZÉ: Is that so? Well, as soon as you got here, a new craving came over me, oh such an awful one.

DUPONT: For what?

ZÉZÉ: *(Tenderly)* I have a craving for you to go!

DUPONT: Huh?

GOLD MEDAL: *(Aside)* Will he fall for it?

DUPONT: *(Disappointed)* Couldn't you have some other craving?

## ACT TWO

ZÉZÉ: If you don't leave right away, I think I'm going to be sick!

DUPONT: *(Extremely agitated, rising and going for his hat, comes back and bumps into* GOLD MEDAL*)* No, no, I'll go... Where would you like me to go?

ZÉZÉ: To Versailles.

DUPONT: Fine, fine, but why?

ZÉZÉ: To buy me asparagus.

DUPONT: Fine, fine. But, listen, there's no reason why I have to buy it way out there in the suburbs.

ZÉZÉ: *(As if she were about to have a nervous breakdown)* He refuses! Ah! My baby! My poor baby is going to have a birthmark!

DUPONT: *(Alarmed)* No, no, lie down! ...Don't do that... I'll go.

ZÉZÉ: Pick out the best they have.

DUPONT: Don't worry... *(Merrily to* GOLD MEDAL*)* She has a craving for asparagus! That's funny. When my mother was carrying me, she had a craving for sour pickles. *(He goes upstage.)*

GOLD MEDAL: *(Aside)* Another craving that went unsatisfied!

DUPONT: *(In ecstasy)* A little Zézé! I've created a little Zézé! *(He exits rapidly U.)*

ZÉZÉ: *(Rising)* Take that stuff off, it's heavy.

GOLD MEDAL: *(Coming down from the stool)* You've got gall!

GOLD MEDAL & ZÉZÉ: *(Singing)* Three cheers for dopes! Three cheers for dopes!

(GOLD MEDAL *and* ZÉZÉ *do a dance. At that moment,* DUPONT *reappears.)*

DUPONT: *(Crying out)* Hey! You're dancing...with that pasta-face?

(GOLD MEDAL *and* ZÉZÉ *stop, petrified.*)

ZÉZÉ: Oh, my dear, it was for sheer joy, the joy of becoming a mother.

DUPONT: *(Suspicious)* Aha. But you were shouting, Three cheers for dopes!

GOLD MEDAL: *(Pretends to wheeze)* Ho...ho...

ZÉZÉ: *(Quickly)* Hopes! Three cheers for hopes of having a baby. So, I was kicking up my heels.

DUPONT: Didn't I tell you not to lift a finger?

GOLD MEDAL: You didn't mention toes.

DUPONT: The old pizza speaks our language?

ZÉZÉ: He speaks it, but he doesn't understand it.

GOLD MEDAL: *Grazie, signor, grazie.*

DUPONT: *(Still suspicious)* All right, all right! I came back to find out how many bunches you wanted.

ZÉZÉ: Just one, my love, just one. But go, go, go!

DUPONT: Yes, yes... *(Aside, going U)* Hmm! Can these characters be pulling a fast one? I intend to find out! *(He exits U.)*

GOLD MEDAL: Hmm! I don't think he trusts me. *(He goes U.)*

ZÉZÉ: Rembrandt? Don't be silly? ...He believes every word I say.

GOLD MEDAL: *(Who has half-opened the door U)* He's gone for good this time. *(He takes off the helmet and toga and places them and the spear U.)*

ZÉZÉ: I could make him believe the moon was shining at high noon.

GOLD MEDAL: Why not? He comes here to get mooned.

# ACT TWO

*(During the next lines* GOLD MEDAL *picks up the easel R, carries it U next to the one already there, and also removes the stools he was sitting and standing on and puts them behind the screen.)*

ZÉZÉ: Oof! Free! I'm free!

MARIETTE: *(Entering U R)* Madame?

ZÉZÉ: What is it, Mariette?

MARIETTE: There's a gentleman been waiting outside for the last few minutes. Since Madame said she'd give Monsieur Rembrandt the bum's rush, I showed the gentleman into the dining room.

ZÉZÉ: Well done, Mariette. Did you ask his name?

MARIETTE: Yes, he said his name was Irrelevant. He's come about the paintings.

ZÉZÉ: Another collector.

GOLD MEDAL: Come to collect the bonus.

ZÉZÉ: *(To* MARIETTE*)* Is he good-looking?

MARIETTE: Pretty classy.

ZÉZÉ: *(To* MARIETTE*)* Well, show him in here. Then come to my room and do my hair.

MARIETTE: Very good, madame.

ZÉZÉ: *(To* GOLD MEDAL, *who has finished rearranging things)* You go in the bathroom and do a water-color.

GOLD MEDAL: I want to watch. *(He pulls a case from his pocket, removes a pipe from it, and puts it in his mouth.)*

ZÉZÉ: No. *(To* MARIETTE*)* Tell him that I'm seeing the Under-Secretary of State for the Fine Arts. That always makes a good impression.

MARIETTE: Yes, madame. And when Monsieur Rembrandt returns?

ZÉZÉ: Tell him to come back tomorrow. Tell him I've had a new craving. The craving to go out of town and kiss my mother. *(She exits D R.)*

MARIETTE: Very good, madame. *(She exits U.)*

GOLD MEDAL: *(To himself)* Good Lord! What I've been through in this dog's life! I've got enough talent to make Rubens turn green, and yet my paintings are signed by a slut! *(He exits U L, after putting the pipe case on the secretary.)*

MARIETTE: *(Showing in* DE TRIVELIN *U R)* This way, monsieur! Madame asked me to tell monsieur that she is seeing the Under-Secretary of State for the Fine Arts.

DE TRIVELIN: Good grief! For how many months now?

MARIETTE: Monsieur doesn't understand...it's not that kind of affair... It's a government commission.

DE TRIVELIN: Ah, I see... *(Slipping her some money)* Here's a gold-piece, tell him to make it snappy.

MARIETTE: Is Monsieur in a hurry?

DE TRIVELIN: You said it!

(MARIETTE *exits while* DE TRIVELIN *sits near the chaise longue.)*

DE TRIVELIN: *(Alone)* Ah! That customs inspector!... *(Rising)* Yesterday, again, just like the day before, just when I was about to you-know-what, his shadow loomed up before me and I heard that snotty voice bawling out, "Anything to declare!" And now it's the last day of the grace period. Only ten hours left! If I haven't recovered my self-confidence by midnight, those unspeakable Duponts will take back my beloved Paulette! So there's no time to lose! Since Couzan's method is supposed to be infallible...let's try it!

*(*ZÉZÉ *appears.)*

# ACT TWO 49

ZÉZÉ: Excuse me for making you wait, monsieur, but I was concluding some business.

DE TRIVELIN: With the Under-Secretary of State for the Fine Arts, I know.

ZÉZÉ: It concerns an important commission for the Luxembourg Museum. *(She gestures to him to sit on the stool while she sits on the chaise longue.)*

DE TRIVELIN: *(After hanging his hat on top of the easel next to the chaise longue)* Madame, I...

ZÉZÉ: *(Altering her tone)* Excuse me! I believe your face is not unknown to me!

DE TRIVELIN: Indeed, madame, I have had the honor of taking supper with you, six months ago.

ZÉZÉ: *(Ransacking her memory)* Wait a minute!

DE TRIVELIN: At a ball given by the Benevolent Brotherhood of Ex-Presidents of the Republic.

ZÉZÉ: Yes, that's right.

DE TRIVELIN: That evening you were delightfully amiable to me. You remarked that I looked like a Watteau.

ZÉZÉ: Watteau! True enough.

DE TRIVELIN: You pinched my arm. You ate orange slices out of my mouth.

ZÉZÉ: *(Laughing)* That sounds like me!

DE TRIVELIN: And when you left, you said: Dear little Watteau, whenever you're in the mood, don't stand on ceremony. It won't cost you a cent!

ZÉZÉ: Ah! That doesn't sound like me! I must have been totally gone, eh?

DE TRIVELIN: Totally gone? No, a brief absence perhaps.

ZÉZÉ: *(Laughing)* That's it. And you never took advantage of the invitation?

DE TRIVELIN: I was away on a trip.

ZÉZÉ: Where to?

DE TRIVELIN: To Whatchmacallit…Timbuktu.

ZÉZÉ: Is it far away?

DE TRIVELIN: Across a great body of water.

ZÉZÉ: Like the Left Bank!

DE TRIVELIN: Yes, but never mind Timbuktu. Ah! Clemency! My Clemency!

ZÉZÉ: Not Clemency—Zézé.

DE TRIVELIN: That's right, Clemency is Couzan.

ZÉZÉ: Couzan?

DE TRIVELIN: Don't try to understand. All you have to know is that I've come here with a heart full of love.

ZÉZÉ: So you thought about me when you were away?

DE TRIVELIN: All the time! I kept thinking: Ah! If only Clemency were here. *(Correcting himself)* Zézé! Zézé! Clemency is Couzan. *(Continuing)* Ah! if only Zézé were here, how I would cuddle her, how I would kiss her!

ZÉZÉ: Isn't he sweet!

DE TRIVELIN: She would restore my self-confidence.

ZÉZÉ: Huh?

DE TRIVELIN: And, with her help, I'd shed my fear of heifers and customs inspectors!

ZÉZÉ: *(Rising)* Heifers and customs inspectors?

DE TRIVELIN: *(Rising)* No, no, don't try to understand. Listen, Zézé, I'll get right to the point. I am a-thirst for love and I have come here to say: Today, I am in the

## ACT TWO

mood. Do you still feel the same way about me as you did six months ago?

ZÉZÉ: A promise is a promise. When Zézé gives her word, she keeps it.

DE TRIVELIN: Ah, Zézé!

ZÉZÉ: Besides, my little Watteau, you're just in time. It's the first day of spring: and I'm a-thirst for love too.

DE TRIVELIN: How do you mean?

ZÉZÉ: You don't expect a woman's cravings to be satisfied by Rembrandt!

DE TRIVELIN: Certainly not, he's been dead for three hundred years!

ZÉZÉ: No, no, not that one.

DE TRIVELIN: There's another one?

ZÉZÉ: Of course there is, my bewildered love. All the "art-collectors" who come here, I stick a painter's name on them...on account of the servants. Rembrandt...

DE TRIVELIN: *(Indicating himself)* Watteau!

ZÉZÉ: Right!

DE TRIVELIN: Most ingenious.

ZÉZÉ: It prevents indiscretion and tittle-tattle.

DE TRIVELIN: The peace of mind of respectable family men, eh?

ZÉZÉ: That's right.

DE TRIVELIN: Well, let's do a Watteau, let's embark for the Isle of Venus.

ZÉZÉ: Hold on. *(With emotion, flinging herself into his arms)* You will be leaving me soon.

DE TRIVELIN: Yes.

ZÉZÉ: When will we meet again? God alone knows!

DE TRIVELIN: Does He? No, He doesn't, I swear He doesn't.

ZÉZÉ: I want you to take away a keepsake of me...a keepsake that you can hang up in your tent out in Timbuktu. *(She takes a painting from the easel U.)*

DE TRIVELIN: A keepsake?

ZÉZÉ: Take this painting.

DE TRIVELIN: Into the bargain! No, that's too much, *(Looking at it)* much too much!

ZÉZÉ: How do you like it?

DE TRIVELIN: *(Looking at the painting upside down)* Very nice!

ZÉZÉ: No, this way! *(She turns it around.)*

DE TRIVELIN: Ah! Delightful! Such freshness of feeling! You can grasp the concept immediately! What's it supposed to be?

ZÉZÉ: It's a subject from ancient legend: the twin founders of Rome, Romulus and Remus.

DE TRIVELIN: Uncle Remus! Oh, it's set in the Deep South!

ZÉZÉ: Two thousand francs, please.

DE TRIVELIN: Two thou... Damn it, that's a scorcher!

ZÉZÉ: Well! My dear, as you say, it is set down South.

DE TRIVELIN: You don't happen to have something that's set at the North Pole? ...A little iceberg, perhaps?

ZÉZÉ: No, but I have more expensive ones.

DE TRIVELIN: *(Quickly)* No thanks! I'll take this one. *(He places the painting on the large easel C, then draws two banknotes from his billfold.)*

ZÉZÉ: You made the right choice. It's the best thing I've ever done.

# ACT TWO

DE TRIVELIN: Here's the two thousand.

ZÉZÉ: Thanks! In time it'll be worth ten thousand if it's worth a penny.

DE TRIVELIN: *If* it's worth a penny.

(MARIETTE *appears.*)

MARIETTE: *(Somewhat embarrassed)* Madame.

ZÉZÉ: What is it?

MARIETTE: *(Coming closer, in an undertone)* Madame's ex would like a word with Madame.

ZÉZÉ: My ex? Which one?

MARIETTE: Monsieur Fragonard!

ZÉZÉ: Fragonard! Oh, it's out of the question right now.

DE TRIVELIN: Absolutely out of the question.

ZÉZÉ: *(Going to* DE TRIVELIN *and putting her arm around his neck, as she speaks to* MARIETTE*)* Tell him I'm with the Under-Secretary of State for the Fine Arts. He'll understand.

MARIETTE: I did tell him. But he insists, he refuses to go away.

ZÉZÉ: What?

MARIETTE: He has only two words to say to Madame, two words of the utmost importance.

ZÉZÉ: Well, if it's only two words... *(To* DE TRIVELIN, *pointing D L)* Watteau, step into the pink boudoir. On a chair you'll find the guest pajamas... I'll be with you in a minute.

DE TRIVELIN: All right, but don't dilly-dally.

ZÉZÉ: Don't worry.

DE TRIVELIN: *(Aside, crossing L)* The things you have to do to be your wife's husband! *(He exits D L.)*

ZÉZÉ: *(To* MARIETTE*)* Mariette, show in Fragonard.

MARIETTE: Very good, madame. *(She exits U R.)*

ZÉZÉ: *(Alone, referring to* DE TRIVELIN*)* I took only two thousand francs, because he's so sweet!...

MARIETTE: *(Entering U R and announcing)* Monsieur Fragonard!

*(*MARIETTE *shows in* LA BAULE *and exits.)*

LA BAULE: *(Entering)* Good afternoon, Zézé!

ZÉZÉ: So, my little Fragonard, what's all this about? You refuse to leave!...

LA BAULE: Don't be annoyed, Zézé! A word, just one word: Is he still here?

ZÉZÉ: Who do you mean?

LA BAULE: The gentleman who arrived half an hour ago.

ZÉZÉ: You know him?...

LA BAULE: I've had him followed for the last two days!

ZÉZÉ: What for?

LA BAULE: For reasons it would take too long to explain. Now, tell me: What does he intend to do here?

ZÉZÉ: Don't be silly! Collect the bonus!

LA BAULE: *(Stupefied)* Impossible!

ZÉZÉ: He's very sweet, but a wee bit eccentric... He keeps making remarks I don't quite understand, about restoring his self-confidence so he won't be afraid of customs inspectors any more.

LA BAULE: *(Aside)* Ah! I understand. *(Aloud)* And have you restored his self-confidence?

ZÉZÉ: No, but he's just about to put on the guest pajamas.

# ACT TWO

LA BAULE: *(Aside)* What a relief! *(Aloud)* Listen, Zézé, would you like to earn five thousand francs?

ZÉZÉ: You bet your life I would!

LA BAULE: Well, the money is yours, on one condition.

ZÉZÉ: Which is?

LA BAULE: That you don't succumb to him for twenty-four hours.

ZÉZÉ: For heaven's sake!

LA BAULE: It's just a whim of mine, don't try to understand it.

ZÉZÉ: But that's...

LA BAULE: *(Interrupting her)* I'll go as high...as high as ten thousand.

ZÉZÉ: Ten thousand?

LA BAULE: Ten thousand.

ZÉZÉ: *(Confused)* It's the first day of spring, you know, and I've got ants in my pants...

LA BAULE: Exercise some pest control, you shameless hussy, and exterminate them! Listen, I'll go as high as fifteen thousand.

ZÉZÉ: Fifteen thousand! Oh, then it's his hard luck!

LA BAULE: It's a deal?

ZÉZÉ: Deal. Just some diddling on the threshold and nothing more until tomorrow.

LA BAULE: As soon as he realizes you're resisting him, he'll try to leave... Prevent him from leaving.

ZÉZÉ: Don't worry, I'll get rid of his clothes.

(ZÉZÉ *rings the bell-buzzer over the window U.*)

LA BAULE: Perfect. And I'll go get the fifteen hundred francs.

ZÉZÉ: *(Quickly)* Pardon me, fifteen thousand.

LA BAULE: All right, only no fooling around.

ZÉZÉ: Of course not.

LA BAULE: *(Aside)* Saved! *(He exits U.)*

ZÉZÉ: Still, it's a pity not to celebrate the spring.

MARIETTE: *(Entering U)* Madame rang?

ZÉZÉ: As soon as Watteau leaves the boudoir, take his clothes and put them in your room.

MARIETTE: Very good, madame.

*(DE TRIVELIN appears D L in pajamas.)*

DE TRIVELIN: Well, Zézé, I'm waiting.

ZÉZÉ: Ah! Doesn't he look cute dressed up like that!

*(MARIETTE exits D L.)*

DE TRIVELIN: The guest pajamas fit me like a glove! *(Sings)* None can compete with me a smidge,
Not even Dalai Lamas,
When I'm all dressed up in my pidge, my pidge,
Dressed up in my pidge-amas.

ZÉZÉ: Are you a poet?

*(MARIETTE reenters D L with DE TRIVELIN's clothes and exits again U L, without his seeing her.)*

DE TRIVELIN: In every man's heart a songwriter lies dormant, but he keeps him bound and gagged. Ah! Zézé, love awaits us. Come! *(He tries to drag her away.)*

ZÉZÉ: *(Pretending to utter a cry of pain)* Ah!

DE TRIVELIN: What?

ZÉZÉ: I've twisted my ankle! ...Ow! Ow!

DE TRIVELIN: Good grief! Lean on me till we get in the other room! *(He indicates D L.)*

ZÉZÉ: Let me sit down!

# ACT TWO

DE TRIVELIN: No, no, don't give in to it.

ZÉZÉ: *(Sitting on the chaise longue)* Only for a second, my dear.

DE TRIVELIN: A second! Ah, that damned ankle is making us lose precious time! Which one is it? *(He sits beside her.)*

ZÉZÉ: I think it's this one, sweetie.

DE TRIVELIN: You aren't sure?

ZÉZÉ: Yes I am! It's this one.

DE TRIVELIN: Wait, I'll massage it gently. *(He massages it.)*

ZÉZÉ: That's lovely!

DE TRIVELIN: *(In a gruff voice)* You ankle you! You deserve a good thrashing.

ZÉZÉ: Huh? *(She tries to withdraw her ankle.)*

DE TRIVELIN: Don't be afraid. I was only trying to scare it so it won't do things like that again!

LA BAULE: *(Sticking his head in the door U; aside, without the others seeing him)* On the sofa? Oh no! *(He disappears.)*

DE TRIVELIN: Ah, how could such a well-turned ankle take a turn for the worse?

ZÉZÉ: It feels better now. Thanks! *(She rises and moves R.)*

DE TRIVELIN: *(Also rising and joining ZÉZÉ, taking her in his arms)* In another moment it'll stop hurting, and, then, to effect a complete cure, I'll smother it with kisses, the way I smother this delicious hand, this divine arm with kisses. *(He kisses her.)*

ZÉZÉ: My, he's a good kisser!

DE TRIVELIN: Ah! Zézé! My Zézé!

ZÉZÉ: Ah! Whoever taught you to kiss like that?

DE TRIVELIN: Nobody! It's in my genes! *(He kisses her again.)*

ZÉZÉ: *(Shutting her eyes)* Watteau! My little Watteau!

DE TRIVELIN: Your skin is so delectable!

ZÉZÉ: *(Her voice dying away)* Ah! You filthy beast! There are only two men in all Paris who know how to kiss a woman, and you're one of them.

DE TRIVELIN: *(Aside)* If only Mama Dupont could hear that!

ZÉZÉ: More! More!

(LA BAULE, *disguised as a female cook with an enormous bosom, stringy blond hair sticking out from under a mobcap, holding a basket and an umbrella, has entered during the last speeches. By gesticulation he expresses his fury and anxiety at seeing* ZÉZÉ *and* DE TRIVELIN *in one another's arms; then he coughs loudly.* DE TRIVELIN *and* ZÉZÉ *pull away from one another.* DE TRIVELIN *moves L.)*

DE TRIVELIN: What on earth is that?

LA BAULE: *(Very cheerfully, in a German accent)* It's chust me, der cook, to get Matame's orders fur mein marketink.

ZÉZÉ: *(Aside, bewildered)* Why, it's Fragonard!

DE TRIVELIN: The hell with her. Give her your orders and send her away!

ZÉZÉ: Yes, darling. *(Undertone to* LA BAULE*)* What are you doing?

LA BAULE: *(Comes D R, undertone)* I'm checking up on you! Is that what you call diddling on the threshold? Why, you shameless hussy, in no time at all he would have beaten down the door and made a forced entry!

# ACT TWO

ZÉZÉ: *(Undertone)* It's a good thing you came in when you did, it was the closest of shaves!

LA BAULE: *(Undertone)* I see that only too well!

ZÉZÉ: What do you expect! It's this darned first day of spring!

LA BAULE: *(Crossing to* DE TRIVELIN*)* Remember the fifteen thousand!

ZÉZÉ: Yes, all right, Gertrude, as far as I'm concerned you can get what you like...

LA BAULE: *(To* DE TRIVELIN*)* Und ass far ass you're gonzerned? *(With concentrated rage)* Pig's head, goose, stuffed tripe, calf's brains, meatball, wild boar...

DE TRIVELIN: Never mind, I'm dining out.

ZÉZÉ: Go away, Gertrude, go away!

LA BAULE: Yah, Matame. *(Curtseying to* DE TRIVELIN*)* Your zervant, monsieur. *(Undertone to* ZÉZÉ*)* Look at what you're putting me through!

ZÉZÉ: *(Undertone)* Don't worry!

LA BAULE: *(To himself)* Ah, but I *am* worrying. I'll keep my eyes peeled! *(He hurries out U.)*

DE TRIVELIN: Gone! Now come and kiss me, my Zézé! *(He tries to kiss her.)*

ZÉZÉ: Just a moment!

DE TRIVELIN: No, I haven't a moment to lose, Father Time is breathing down my neck.

ZÉZÉ: If I were to give myself to you just like that, right away, off the cuff, what would you think of me?

DE TRIVELIN: That you were my Clemency!

ZÉZÉ: *(Put out)* That Clemency again!

DE TRIVELIN: *(Recovering quickly)* The clemency of heaven! The promised land so ardently desired...the beacon that guides the seaman—in distress... Be my beacon! Come and drown me in your glow in the pink boudoir! *(He tries to drag* ZÉZÉ *to it.)*

ZÉZÉ: Wait twenty-four hours!

DE TRIVELIN: *(Giving a start)* Twenty-four hours? Is that the answer you make to a drowning man: I'll fish you out in twenty-four hours? To the poor creature dying of thirst: Next week I'll send you a bottle of seltzer?

ZÉZÉ: Twenty-four hours is the minimal delay any decent woman can make before giving in.

DE TRIVELIN: And that was why you had me put on the guest pajamas? Ask for my blood, my life, but not that, not that!

ZÉZÉ: But twenty-four hours is tomorrow!

DE TRIVELIN: You're telling *me*! Tomorrow will be too late, I'm leaving at once for Timbuktu!

ZÉZÉ: So you'll miss your train.

DE TRIVELIN: But if I miss it once more, I'm a ruined man! Tomorrow it's going out of service. *(Taking her in his arms)* Look, Zézé, you can't be serious: we are both a-thirst for love, while the fountainhead is bubbling in your bedroom. *(He indicates the boudoir.)*

ZÉZÉ: *(Fending him off)* The fountain won't dry up while you wait!

DE TRIVELIN: There are some fountains you mustn't keep waiting! Didn't you tell me you had ants in your pants!

ZÉZÉ: *(Quickly and very passionately)* Don't bring them up!

DE TRIVELIN: Have they beat a retreat?

ZÉZÉ: Just the opposite, they're starting to dance a fandango!

# ACT TWO

DE TRIVELIN: Well then, let's follow their example. *(He kisses her.)*

ZÉZÉ: *(Giving in more and more)* No, no!

DE TRIVELIN: Yes! Yes! Isn't today the first day of spring?

ZÉZÉ: Shut up! Shut up!

DE TRIVELIN: And a Friday to boot—Venus's day!

ZÉZÉ: *(About to give in)* Springtime *and* Venus's day!

DE TRIVELIN: *(Taking her in his arms, kissing her)* Love is in the air, love is all around.

ZÉZÉ: *(Weakening)* It's in the air, it's all around.

DE TRIVELIN: And are we to put it off until tomorrow?

ZÉZÉ: *(Pulling away with a cry)* To hell with the money! Never let it be said that on Venus's day Zézé didn't celebrate the coming of spring. Let's go! *(She exits D L.)*

DE TRIVELIN: *(Triumphantly)* At last!

(DE TRIVELIN *pushes* ZÉZÉ *into the room L. At that moment* LA BAULE *appears at the door U. He is dressed as a customs inspector as in* ACT ONE. DE TRIVELIN *notices him as he turns to go out L, utters a cry, and stops aghast.* LA BAULE *takes several steps towards him, holding up his hand.)*

DE TRIVELIN: *(Babbling in ludicrous terror)* The phantom of that cust…cust…customs inspector.

LA BAULE: *(Disguising his voice as in* ACT ONE*)* Anything to declare?

DE TRIVELIN: *(In ludicrous terror, moving R, his back to the audience)* Don't! Don't!

(LA BAULE, *walking backwards, reaches U L, stops a few steps from the door, not taking his eyes off the trembling* DE TRIVELIN.*)*

LA BAULE: *(As above, only louder)* Have you anything to declare?

DE TRIVELIN: Ah!

(DE TRIVELIN *turns his head to keep from seeing* LA BAULE, *who takes advantage of this to disappear U L.*)

(DE TRIVELIN *gradually turns his head, fails to see* LA BAULE, *rushes to the door U L, opens it quickly, then closes it and comes back C.*)

DE TRIVELIN: *(With ludicrous fury)* What's going on? More hallucinations!...

ZÉZÉ: *(Entering D L, undressed, in a petticoat and underbodice, very passionately)* Well, my little Watteau?

DE TRIVELIN: *(As if waking from a dream, his arms dangling)* Huh? What?

ZÉZÉ: Are you coming?

DE TRIVELIN: Where to?

ZÉZÉ: The fountainhead!

DE TRIVELIN: No thanks! *(Shaking his head)* I'm not thirsty any more!

ZÉZÉ: Huh?

DE TRIVELIN: *(Aside)* This time I *am* done for!

ZÉZÉ: *(Coming to him)* What are you talking about? Just now you were kissing me and begging me to love you and prattling about springtime!

DE TRIVELIN: *(Piteously)* The season's over!

ZÉZÉ: Just like that?

(DE TRIVELIN *nods yes.*)

ZÉZÉ: So it's autumn now?

DE TRIVELIN: *(Hanging his head)* Worse!

ZÉZÉ: Winter?

# ACT TWO

DE TRIVELIN: A blizzard! The Seine is frozen over! ...I'd better go. *(He goes to get his hat and the painting he bought from the easel C. He puts on his hat and goes U. ZÉZÉ runs after him and brings him back by force.)*

ZÉZÉ: Come on now! Let you go like that without celebrating the first day of spring!

DE TRIVELIN: You mean, you don't hold it against me?

*(DE TRIVELIN clasps ZÉZÉ in his arms, holding her between himself and the painting which he hasn't dropped. During the next speeches, he gradually raises the painting.)*

ZÉZÉ: *(Still very passionate, rubbing up against him)* It's only overexcitement. Very flattering for a woman... just calm down, silly boy, my hand hasn't lost its cunning...I am summertime, scorching summertime, the dog days that melt down frost and icicles.

DE TRIVELIN: *(Gradually becoming aroused)* Zézé!

ZÉZÉ: Look at these greedy lips calling for kisses.

DE TRIVELIN: Yes.

ZÉZÉ: Look at these white shoulders calling for caresses!

DE TRIVELIN: *(Aroused)* Yes! Yes!

ZÉZÉ: Look! Look!

DE TRIVELIN: I'm all eyes! I'm all eyes!

ZÉZÉ: Now tell me what winter can resist the warmth of these arms?

DE TRIVELIN: Nary a one... Nary a one!

ZÉZÉ: Then thaw is setting in!

DE TRIVELIN: Totally.

ZÉZÉ: And springtime has returned!

DE TRIVELIN: *(Gleefully)* It has.

ZÉZÉ: *(Triumphant, pulling away from him)* Aha! I knew it!

DE TRIVELIN: But springtime doesn't last forever. Quick, before it skedaddles!

*(He draws her towards the D L door. They disappear out the door.* DUPONT *appears U R, followed by* MARIETTE.*)*

MARIETTE: But, Monsieur, there's no point in coming in. Madame isn't here, she's gone to kiss her mother.

DUPONT: *(Goes to open the door D L, then closes it again)* Another craving!

MARIETTE: Yes, monsieur.

DUPONT: I can just picture her mother! She wears checked pants and has a beard a foot long!

MARIETTE: Monsieur would be wiser to come back tomorrow.

DUPONT: *(Aside)* I think I'd better play up to this girl. *(Aloud)* Mariette!

MARIETTE: Monsieur Rembrandt?

DUPONT: Listen. I'm fed up with Zézé. I like your looks. How would you like twenty-five hundred a month and a little backstairs flat?

MARIETTE: *(Clasping her hands in glee)* Oh! Monsieur Rembrandt!

DUPONT: But on one condition: don't conceal anything from me.

MARIETTE: *(Unbuttoning her blouse)* I never will.

DUPONT: Not that, that's for later. *(She buttons up her blouse.)* Don't conceal anything from me concerning Zézé.

MARIETTE: Ah? All right!

DUPONT: Her cravings?

MARIETTE: A gimmick for getting rid of Monsieur.

DUPONT: So she's two-timing me?

MARIETTE: With men of all ages. Old ones and brand-new ones!

DUPONT: I'm a cuckold!

MARIETTE: Up to your eyebrows! As for her painting, she's never touched a brush.

DUPONT: No?

MARIETTE: There's a down-and-out Gold Medal winner who does her paintings. The one that played the model.

DUPONT: *(Stalking about in a rage)* Old Patsy Defool? I'll be damned! Double damnation!

MARIETTE: *(Stopping him)* Don't get so hot and bothered since you're fed up with her and we're going to move in together. *(She tries to put her arms around his neck.)*

DUPONT: *(Pushing her away)* The two of us? Oh no, you've got another think coming, my good girl!

MARIETTE: Huh! You said that to make me talk!

DUPONT: Right the first time! But things aren't over just like that. *(Going to the door D R and opening it)* I'm going to plump myself down right here. *(Noticing the palette on the stool near the door)* And the first person to come in'll get this in his face! *(He disappears D R.)*

MARIETTE: *(Alone)* Ah! The old creep! He conned me. Well, I guess I'd better start looking for another job.

(MARIETTE *goes U, but* DE TRIVELIN *appears D L, and, at the sound of the door,* MARIETTE *turns around;* DE TRIVELIN, *his painting under his arm, but without his hat, quietly closes the door and strides the forestage twice in delirious joy.)*

DE TRIVELIN: *(In an undertone)* I've done it! I've done it! I've done it! She's napping...I'll take the opportunity to make my escape.

MARIETTE: Monsieur Watteau!

DE TRIVELIN: *(Brimming over with joy)* Ah, Mariette! My little Mariette!

MARIETTE: I can see monsieur is satisfied.

DE TRIVELIN: Satisfied? All the customs inspectors in the world can gang up on me, but I'm not afraid!

MARIETTE: Ah!

DE TRIVELIN: I've recovered my confidence, I've recovered my self-respect, I've recovered everything except my clothes. Where are they?

MARIETTE: *(Embarrassed)* I don't know, monsieur.

DE TRIVELIN: What do you mean, you don't know? They were here and now they're not. *(He points D L.)*

MARIETTE: But, monsieur...

DE TRIVELIN: A hundred francs if you bring them here this instant.

MARIETTE: Ah! Then I'll get them for you. *(Aside)* Oh well, what difference does it make now! *(She exits D R.)*

DE TRIVELIN: *(Alone, going U)* Ah! Paulette! My adorable Lélette, I'll be your husband before midnight! *(He opens the door U and suddenly slams it shut.)* Great howling crash-wagons! My mother-in-law with La Baule! If they find me in pajamas, I'm ruined! *(He rapidly hides behind the screen.)*

LA BAULE: *(Rushing in through the entrance door, followed by* MME DUPONT, *whose hand he is holding)* This way, dear lady, this way quickly!

MME DUPONT: But, my dear La Baule, why won't you tell me where you're taking me?

# ACT TWO

LA BAULE: This is a harlot's house!

MME DUPONT: *(Indignant)* A harlot! What are we doing here?

LA BAULE: Catching your son-in-law in the act.

MME DUPONT: My son-in-law!

LA BAULE: Yes, your son-in-law has been here for an hour.

DE TRIVELIN: *(Sticking his head over the screen; aside)* The bastard!

MME DUPONT: *(Crossing L)* Hell's bells and little fishes! He behaves like a eunuch in his own house while he's gallivanting around with floozies. Where is he?

LA BAULE: In my lady's chamber, no doubt. *(He indicates the room D R.)*

MME DUPONT: Give me your cane! La Baule, give me your cane.

LA BAULE: With pleasure.

*(LA BAULE hands it to MME DUPONT.)*

MME DUPONT: Thanks! I'm going to break this cane over the posterior of the last of the De Trivelins.

LA BAULE: Be my guest!

MME DUPONT: Ah! You villain, so this is why you've got nothing to declare! *(She heads for ZÉZÉ's room.)*

LA BAULE: *(Sitting on the chair)* I believe I'll take a box-seat!

DE TRIVELIN: *(Aside)* Swine!

*(Barely has MME DUPONT entered when terrible shouts can be heard offstage.)*

LA BAULE: *(With satisfaction, indicating D R)* It's heating up in there!

*(The D R door flies open, and* DUPONT *appears with his hat caved in.* MME DUPONT *is behind the door, trying to get in. The door keeps opening and closing. Finally,* DUPONT *crouches before the door and keeps* MME DUPONT *from coming in. During this business,* LA BAULE *has risen in bewilderment.)*

DUPONT: *(In a panic)* My wife! it's my wife!

LA BAULE: *(Dumbfounded)* Ah! Monsieur Dupont!

DUPONT: *(Ditto)* La Baule!

DE TRIVELIN: *(Aside)* My father-in-law!

LA BAULE: You, at Zézé's!

DUPONT: She's an old friend of mine!

LA BAULE: I'll be damned!

DE TRIVELIN: *(Aside)* So *he's* Rembrandt!

MME DUPONT'S VOICE: *(Offstage)* Miserable wretch! Renegade!

LA BAULE: Hide.

DUPONT: Take my place and tell her I've gone.

LA BAULE: Hurry up.

*(*LA BAULE *comes and leans up against the door in* DUPONT's *place.)*

DUPONT: Where can I hide? *(Panic-stricken, he grabs a huge painting leaning against the easel C. and hides behind it, so that the painting seems to be placed on an easel. This painting depicts a life-sized, scantily clad woman.)*

DUPONT: *(Hidden behind the painting)* Open the door!

*(*LA BAULE *opens the door.* MME DUPONT *appears, her hat askew, and plants a slap on* LA BAULE.*)*

LA BAULE: *(Shouts)* Ow!

MME DUPONT: You're not him, where is he? Where is he? I'll polish him off!

# ACT TWO

(MME DUPONT *moves L, followed by* LA BAULE; *then she turns around. We see that her right cheek is smeared with paint: red, blue, black, yellow.*)

LA BAULE: *(Uttering a cry of amazement at seeing her face)* Ah!

MME DUPONT: Tell me, will you!

LA BAULE: He's gone!

MME DUPONT: The coward ran away, but he's just postponing the day of judgment. *(She starts for the U R door.)*

LA BAULE: *(Trying to hold her back)* Madame Dupont, listen to me.

MME DUPONT: *(Pushing him away)* Let go of me, you… But thanks all the same for bringing me here to nab my husband!

DUPONT: *(Aside, his head popping out from behind the painting)* Huh!

LA BAULE: *(Trying to hold her back)* Madame Dupont! Madame Dupont!

MME DUPONT: *(Pushing him away)* Let go of me!

(MME DUPONT *exits U, brandishing pieces of* LA BAULE's *walking stick.*)

LA BAULE: *(Falling on to the seat of the chair C)* I'm flabbergasted! Flabbergasted!

*(Barely has* MME DUPONT *gone, when* DUPONT *leans the painting against the easel, leaps on* LA BAULE, *and slaps him.* LA BAULE *cries out.)*

DUPONT: *(Grabbing* LA BAULE *by the coat collar, forcing him to rise and shaking him furiously)* Aha! So you were the one who brought my wife here to nab me!

LA BAULE: *(Half-choked)* Monsieur Dupont!

DUPONT: *(Shaking him)* You contemptible twit! I'll skin you alive!

LA BAULE: You're strangling me.

DUPONT: I don't give a damn!

(DE TRIVELIN, *his head above the screen, watches this scene and splits his sides laughing.*)

DUPONT: After I made you first in line!

LA BAULE: *(Managing to get loose)* I did bring Madame Dupont here, I admit it, but it was to nab De Trivelin!

DUPONT: What's that? My son-in-law is here?

LA BAULE: Yes. How could I suspect that you were Zézé's lover as well?

DUPONT: All the same, my wife surprised me in Zézé's boudoir.

LA BAULE: *(Struck by an idea)* Oh! Tell her that you came here to catch De Trivelin too!

DUPONT: Good idea!

LA BAULE: I'll tell her that I was the one who alerted you.

DUPONT: Saved! Paulette shall be yours again. First let me catch up with my wife and I'll be right back... *(He quickly vanishes U.)*

LA BAULE: *(Back turned to the screen)* I've got to find out what happened to the other one.

(DE TRIVELIN *leans over the screen and sends him a resounding slap; then he comes out from the screen and goes D R of* LA BAULE, *who is rubbing his cheek.*)

LA BAULE: *(Startled)* Him! It's him!

DE TRIVELIN: Yes, it is.

LA BAULE: *(Furious)* Monsieur de Trivelin!

DE TRIVELIN: *(Continuing)* I heard it all, I know it all!

LA BAULE: *(Aside)* Good grief!

DE TRIVELIN: So! You had me followed! So! You were trying to get me nabbed?

LA BAULE: Well, yes, I did...I loathe you, I detest you, I swore you would never be my Paulette's husband!

DE TRIVELIN: We shall see about that. I still have until midnight.

LA BAULE: *(Sneering)* Ha! Ha! *(Furious)* As for those slaps, I demand satisfaction.

DE TRIVELIN: You'll get it, but first I have to retrieve my clothes...I'll go look for them myself. *(He exits U R.)*

LA BAULE: *(Alone, on the verge of tears)* Slapped by father, mother, son-in-law, the whole family! Ah! Paulette! My Paulette, haven't I suffered enough to win you! *(He moves U.)*

MARIETTE: *(Entering U L with* DE TRIVELIN's *clothes. When he hears the door,* LA BAULE *turns around.)* Here are the clothes!

LA BAULE: What clothes?

MARIETTE: The ones that belong to the gent in pajamas.

LA BAULE: *(Quickly)* Ah! Hand them over!

MARIETTE: But, Monsieur...

LA BAULE: Hand them over, you little wretch, or I'll jump your bones. *(He snatches* DE TRIVELIN's *clothes.)*

MARIETTE: *(Running L)* He's a sex fiend!

LA BAULE: *(Struck by an idea)* The sex fiend! *(Slapping the clothes in his rage.)* Ah! I'll phone the police and get him arrested as the Vincennes sex fiend! *(He runs off U, carrying* DE TRIVELIN's *clothes with him.)*

MARIETTE: *(Alone)* Hey! What about my money!

DE TRIVELIN: *(Entering U R, to himself)* I can't seem to lay my hands on… *(Noticing* MARIETTE*)* Ah! There she is! Where are my clothes?

MARIETTE: Why, monsieur, I haven't got them anymore.

DE TRIVELIN: Who does?

MARIETTE: The gent who brought the old lady.

DE TRIVELIN: *(Furious)* And you let him take them!

MARIETTE: But, monsieur, he took them by force. *(Holding out her hand)* The hundred francs?

DE TRIVELIN: Listen, you'll get two hundred, if you can procure me some clothes.

MARIETTE: Cash down.

DE TRIVELIN: But my wallet's in my coat!

MARIETTE: Then, goodnight. You can't catch me with that trick twice. *(She exits U.)*

DE TRIVELIN: *(Going to the window and opening it)* Oh, great! Ah! La Baule, you bastard, you'll pay for this. *(Looking out the window.)* There he is, crossing the street! And not a car in sight to run him over! How can I get some clothes? Time is running out… Oh, here's an idea! *(Leans out the window and calls offstage.)* Hey! You there! Monsieur… Hey, monsieur! …Yes, I'm talking to you!

FRONTIGNAC'S VOICE: What do you want, monsieur?

DE TRIVELIN: In heaven's name, come up here right away. The mezzanine, the door on the left.

FRONTIGNAC'S VOICE: What for, monsieur?

DE TRIVELIN: I can't shout it out the window, but you can save my life.

FRONTIGNAC'S VOICE: All right…I'm coming.

## ACT TWO

DE TRIVELIN: *(Closing the window)* He's coming… thank God! Except, somebody I don't know will never willingly consent to hand over his clothes…I'll get nowhere begging him…I need a weapon to back up my pleas. *(Noticing on the secretary L the pipe case that Gold Medal left there, and picking it up rapidly.)* A revolver! *(He opens the case.)* No! it's a pipe case

*(Seeing the door open and* FRONTIGNAC *appear)*

DE TRIVELIN: There he is! Oh well! *(He hides the pipe case behind his back.)*

FRONTIGNAC: *(Entering U)* Here I am, monsieur, I found the door open.

DE TRIVELIN: *(Going U)* Come in, monsieur, come in! *(He has him cross L.)*

FRONTIGNAC: How can I be of service to you?

DE TRIVELIN: Take off all your clothes and give them to me.

FRONTIGNAC: *(Dumbfounded)* What, you had me come up here to ask me to…

DE TRIVELIN: Monsieur, I am armed and will not hesitate to commit a crime. *(He rapidly displays the pipe case in his hand.)*

FRONTIGNAC: *(Quickly, frightened)* Put it away!

DE TRIVELIN: Gladly. *(He conceals it behind his back.)*

FRONTIGNAC: Monsieur, you can't be serious.

DE TRIVELIN: Somebody stole my clothes…

FRONTIGNAC: But I had nothing to do with it.

DE TRIVELIN: One…two…three. *(He aims the pipe case at him.)*

FRONTIGNAC: *(Frightened)* Put it away, put it away. *(While removing his trousers)* Ah! What an adventure! … Asking people to come upstairs…

DE TRIVELIN: Speed it up, monsieur, I'm in a hurry. Your trousers?

FRONTIGNAC: *(Handing them to him)* Here!

DE TRIVELIN: Thanks.

FRONTIGNAC: This is crazy! Incredible!

DE TRIVELIN: *(Who has put the trousers on over his pajamas, still holding the pipe case)* Now your coat and vest, quick!

FRONTIGNAC: But, monsieur, it takes time.

DE TRIVELIN: I have only five hours and fifty minutes.

FRONTIGNAC: To do what? *(He throws him his coat and vest.)*

DE TRIVELIN: None of your business. Where can I send this back to you?

FRONTIGNAC: Frontignac! Grand Hotel!

DE TRIVELIN: Good! Your hat...

FRONTIGNAC: *(Handing it to him)* Unbelievable! Preposterous!

DE TRIVELIN: Thanks. *(Putting the pipe case into his hand.)* Here, this is for you.

FRONTIGNAC: *(Uttering a shout of joy, thinking he has a revolver)* Ah!

DE TRIVELIN: *(Aside)* And now let's beat it down the back stairs. *(He exits quickly U R.)*

FRONTIGNAC: Ah! You scoundrel! You're going to give me back my clothes! *(Opening the case)* What in the world is this? A pipe case! Oh, for heaven's sake!

*(DUPONT appears U.)*

DUPONT: *(Seeing FRONTIGNAC from behind and thinking that he is DE TRIVELIN)* Now it's your turn, Trivelin. *(He leaps on him and shakes him.)*

# ACT TWO

FRONTIGNAC: Hey! Help! *(He turns around.)*

DUPONT: *(Startled)* The camel dealer in his underwear!

FRONTIGNAC: *(Ditto)* Monsieur Dupont!

DUPONT: What are you doing in this state of undress?

FRONTIGNAC: Someone brought me up here and made off with my clothes.

DUPONT: Come, come! Do you think I'm going to swallow a story that size! How come I caught you in your underwear in my mistress's house?

FRONTIGNAC: Huh? Is that where I am?

DUPONT: Yes, monsieur, in my sweetie's house, and she's two-timing me with you the way she two-timed me with others, because I'm a cuckold!

FRONTIGNAC: I'd be surprised if you were anything else. But it's got nothing to do with me.

DUPONT: Tell it to the marines, monsieur!

FRONTIGNAC: *(Struck by an idea)* Anyway, I couldn't care less whether you believe me or not. I still have 195 Duponts to cover. Hand over your clothes.

DUPONT: Huh?

FRONTIGNAC: No shilly-shallying. I'm armed. *(He threatens him with the pipe case.)*

DUPONT: *(Scared within an inch of his life)* Please, put it away!

FRONTIGNAC: With pleasure. *(He conceals it behind his back.)* Your clothes or do I blow your brains out?

DUPONT: But, monsieur...

FRONTIGNAC: Ready, aim, fire! *(He gestures with the pipe case.)*

DUPONT: *(Panicked)* Put it away! Put it away! *(While taking off his trousers)* Oh, this is awful!

FRONTIGNAC: Your trousers!

DUPONT: *(Tossing them over)* Here they are!

FRONTIGNAC: Thanks. *(He puts them on.)* And your vest! Now the coat!

DUPONT: You need that too?...

FRONTIGNAC: On the double! ...Or else...

DUPONT: *(Removing his vest and coat)* If I saw this on stage I'd never believe it!

FRONTIGNAC: Quick! Quick! Hand it over.

DUPONT: All right! Cutthroat. *(He hands them over.)*

FRONTIGNAC: *(While dressing)* Don't come any closer.

DUPONT: *(Grumbling)* Camel dealer! You give *me* the hump!

FRONTIGNAC: Your hat. (DUPONT *gives it to him.*) Thanks—a bit snug, but that's not important.

DUPONT: *(Snide)* You need anything else?

FRONTIGNAC: *(Coming out from behind the table)* Not at the moment. I'll send it all back to you. Meanwhile, this is for you. *(He puts the pipe case in his hand.)*

DUPONT: *(Thinking he has the revolver and threatening him by rushing at him)* Ah! you wretch! Now you're going to give me back...

FRONTIGNAC: *(Smiling)* Don't get excited, it's a pipe case.

DUPONT: Huh?

FRONTIGNAC: I was fooled myself a minute ago.

DUPONT: *(Furious)* Ah! Honestly!

FRONTIGNAC: So long, Dupont! *(He heads for the D R door and opens it.)* This isn't the way out.

## ACT TWO

DUPONT: *(Quickly shoving him off D R.)* Yes it is! *(Bolting the door shut.)* Ah! Now I've got you... That room has no other exit... You won't get away from me! *(Noticing* ZÉZÉ, *who appears D L.)*

ZÉZÉ: *(To herself)* What happened to Watteau?

DUPONT: *(Thundering)* Madame!

ZÉZÉ: *(Uttering a cry of surprise)* Ah! Rembrandt in his underwear!

DUPONT: Yes, Rembrandt, whom you didn't expect to see so soon.

ZÉZÉ: As a matter of fact, my love, I thought you were in Versailles buying me asparagus!

DUPONT: *(Exploding)* Asparagus! Ha! I'll give you asparagus!

GOLD MEDAL: *(Entering U L)* Hey! What's all the racket? *(Stopping short at the sight of* DUPONT*)* Uh oh!

DUPONT: *(Aside)* The phony Patsy Dafool!

GOLD MEDAL: Did you bring the asparagus? Lemme have it! *(He turns around.)*

DUPONT: Here it is. *(He kicks him.)*

GOLD MEDAL & ZÉZÉ: *(Together)* Huh?

DUPONT: You unspeakable paint-slinger, in the pay of a tramp who's never held a brush in her life.

ZÉZÉ: *(Aside)* The beans are spilled.

GOLD MEDAL: *(Furious)* Who are you calling a paint-slinger?

DUPONT: Are you two done double-crossing me?

ZÉZÉ: This is plenty, thanks. Gold Medal, take down that Rembrandt.

GOLD MEDAL: Right. *(To* DUPONT*)* Are you going to beat it and in two shakes?

DUPONT: Yes, I'll beat it, but not before confronting Madame with one of the many lovers she's been two-timing me with. *(He opens the door to* FRONTIGNAC's *room.)* Come out, camel jockey!

FRONTIGNAC: *(Appearing)* At last!

ZÉZÉ: *(Shrieking when she sees* FRONTIGNAC*)* Ah!

FRONTIGNAC: *(Shouting when he sees* ZÉZÉ*)* Ah!

ZÉZÉ: My husband!

FRONTIGNAC: My wife!

DUPONT: *(Stupefied)* What did he say?

FRONTIGNAC: And she's Dupont's mistress!

GOLD MEDAL: *(Aside)* Ha! This is neat!

DUPONT: His wife! She's his wife! *(He tries to sit down but falls along with the chair, knocking over the stool and the paintbox beside him.)*

FRONTIGNAC: At last I'll be able to get a divorce!

*(*GOLD MEDAL *is in stitches.)*

MARIETTE: *(Entering)* Madame! Madame! A Police Inspector's here…

ALL: An Inspector!

FRONTIGNAC: *(Jovially)* Just in the nick of time.

MARIETTE: He says that the Vincennes sex fiend is hiding here in his underwear.

ALL: Huh?

INSPECTOR: *(Enters followed by two* POLICEMEN *Where is he? (Noticing* DUPONT*)* Ah! There he is. *(To the* POLICEMEN*)* Arrest that man.

*(The* POLICEMEN *collar* DUPONT.*)*

DUPONT: *(Roaring)* Will you let go of me? I'm Dupont, Judge Dupont!..

*(The* POLICEMEN *lead out a struggling* DUPONT. *The other characters are prostrate with laughter.)*

*(Tableau)*

## END ACT TWO

# ACT THREE

(*Same setting as* ACT ONE)

COUZAN: (*Entering U C followed by* ERNESTINE) Is Judge Dupont at home?

ERNESTINE: No, monsieur... The master got up early to go to court.

COUZAN: (*In an undertone, moving R*) Hmm! I'd have thought it more likely he'd leave court early to get it up.

ERNESTINE: Beg pardon?

COUZAN: Never mind! ...What about Monsieur de Trivelin?

ERNESTINE: Went out about two o'clock.

COUZAN: And Madame Dupont?

ERNESTINE: Monsieur La Baule came to fetch her about ten minutes ago. They flew out of here like a whirlwind. As for the Countess, she's reading in her room.

COUZAN: (*Moving L*) How about Mademoiselle Lise?

ERNESTINE: She's at her piano lesson.

GONTRAN: (*Entering U C with an unframed painting wrapped in newspaper*) Good afternoon, Monsieur Couzan.

(ERNESTINE *exits.*)

COUZAN: Ah! You can keep me company. How are you?

GONTRAN: *(Setting the painting on the table)* A gift for my father-in-law-to-be.

COUZAN: It's easy to see you're engaged!

GONTRAN: Ah, Monsieur Dupont will be so pleased. He's been asking for it!

COUZAN: *(Indicating the painting)* For this?

GONTRAN: Not exactly... The day before yesterday—the day after the newlyweds came back from their honeymoon—my father-in-law-to-be asked me to bring him proof that I was capable of making a woman happy.

COUZAN: My, my! He's taking his precautions.

GONTRAN: And when I expressed my astonishment, he said, I won't have Lise shortchanged by her husband the way her sister was by hers.

COUZAN: He's telling everyone about it! ...And did you obey his injunction? *(He sits on the ottoman.)*

GONTRAN: *(Indignant)* Monsieur Couzan, I adore my fiancée, and I would never cheat on her for anything in the world.

COUZAN: So?

GONTRAN: Now look! ...When a person wants a church wedding, he can obtain a testimonial of confession without going to confession! ...Well, yesterday afternoon I looked up one of those ladies whose special mission is the happiness of men.

COUZAN: And the lady presented you with a testimonial?

GONTRAN: Of good misconduct... *(Pulling a paper out of his pocket and reading)* "I certify that Monsieur Gontran

## ACT THREE

des Barbettes has been my lover and I have nothing but praise for him in all respects... He is the paragon of passion."

COUZAN: No less!

GONTRAN: *(Reading)* "To try him is to buy him."

COUZAN: *(Laughing)* And how much did she charge you for that?

GONTRAN: Since she combines sex and painting, she merely asked me to buy one of her works. Here it is! *(He removes the wrapping from the painting.)*

COUZAN: Indeed! What have we here? *(Looking at the painting* GONTRAN *displays)* It's a Zézé!

GONTRAN: Has she got any talent?

COUZAN: Talents plural.

GONTRAN: I plan to offer this painting to my father-in-law-to-be, since he's a collector! ...I bet he'll be surprised.

COUZAN: I can guarantee it! Nevertheless, I'm going to give you a magic word. If he ever loses his temper with you, if he ever gives you a hard time, the thing that will muzzle him forever is to raise your finger like so and say this one word: Rembrandt!

GONTRAN: Rembrandt?

COUZAN: Yes, and now come with me to his study. We'll find a proper spot to hang this painting...

GONTRAN: Rembrandt? *(He exits U L, carrying the painting.)*

COUZAN: Rembrandt. *(Alone)* I was sure Zézé was a tart.

PAULETTE: *(Entering D R with a book)* Good afternoon, godfather.

COUZAN: *(Crossing D)* Good afternoon, my sweet. *(He kisses her.)* Anything new since yesterday?

PAULETTE: Not that I know of, godfather.

COUZAN: Ah! *(Aside)* He hasn't done it yet!

PAULETTE: Why do you ask?

COUZAN: No reason, my sweet. Go on with your reading, don't bother about me...I plan to join Des Barbettes in the study. We're preparing a surprise for your father.

PAULETTE: You're always looking for ways to make people happy.

COUZAN: *(On his way out)* Why not? It's my nature! *(He exits U L.)*

PAULETTE: Now where did I leave off? *(She sits on the sofa and reads.)* "Fanny was already in bed when Léon entered the bridal chamber. `Alone at last!' he exclaimed, as he drew near the bed; then he slipped in beside Fanny, who was panting and blushing...and the great mystery was consummated; the awesome and delectable mystery... At last Fanny knew the meaning of love..." *(Spoken, dreamily)* The great mystery, awesome and delectable!

LISE: *(Entering U C, in a hat, with sheet music under her arm)* I'm back! What, you're all alone? *(She puts the sheet music on the furniture L of the U C door.)*

PAULETTE: Yes.

LISE: Isn't Gontran here?

PAULETTE: He's in Papa's study with Couzan.

LISE: *(Crosses R of the sofa and sits next to* PAULETTE*)* Oh! If he's with Couzan, he can certainly wait five minutes... Besides, now we can have a nice little chat...

PAULETTE: Do you have something to tell me, Lisette?

# ACT THREE

LISE: No, but you have something to tell me! Now's the chance to keep your promise.

PAULETTE: What promise?

LISE: The night before your wedding you promised to tell me all about it.

PAULETTE: All about what?

LISE: Your wedding night, don't you remember?

PAULETTE: Oh! There wasn't anything very special about that, darling! ...You imagine all sorts of things beforehand, but there's nothing to it!

LISE: Nothing?

PAULETTE: Of course not, darling...it's the same as before, except, instead of being alone in bed, there are two of you. That's all!

LISE: *(Furious, rising)* That isn't true! I know it isn't true!

PAULETTE: I swear it!

LISE: That isn't very nice of you! You're all like that! ... The night before, you promise to tell everything; and the next day, a person can't get anything out of you!

PAULETTE: Lisette, I swear I'm telling you the truth!

LISE: Sure! sure! When my girlfriend Marcelle got married, she swore to tell me everything too. The next day she looked radiant...and when I reminded her of her promise, she started to make up some fib...oh! what a fib...and refused to tell me anything either...

PAULETTE: Because there was nothing to tell!

LISE: Oh sure, but I subtly managed to worm something out of her just the same.

PAULETTE: And what did she say?

LISE: She said, "My dear, expect everything and don't be surprised by anything."

PAULETTE: That's what she said?

LISE: And she added, with downcast eyes: "It's a great mystery."

PAULETTE: *(Quickly)* A great mystery! She said a great mystery?

LISE: An awesome and delectable mystery.

PAULETTE: Like in the novel.

LISE: What novel?

PAULETTE: A novel Mama forbade me to read before I was married. I got it out of the library.

LISE: Ah! Then, you see, there is a mystery.

PAULETTE: But I don't know what it is, I swear I don't.

LISE: Really and truly? And you've been married five weeks? For all your promises, you won't tell me a thing, and on my wedding night, when I'm alone with my husband, I'll look like a dummy.

PAULETTE: Lise!

(COUZAN *appears U L.*)

COUZAN: Why, what's the matter?

LISE: The matter is that Paulette is the world's worst sister. *(She exits D L.)*

COUZAN: My word! What can have happened?

PAULETTE: *(A bit edgy)* Godfather, godfather dear, you're a mature man, a man of experience, a married man?

COUZAN: For twenty years!

PAULETTE: Well then, tell me candidly, no beating about the bush. What is getting married all about?

COUZAN: Getting married?

PAULETTE: Yes.

# ACT THREE

COUZAN: Well...there're charming ceremonies, first a civil one and then a religious one...with a splendid banquet to finish it off.

PAULETTE: Yes...yes...I know...and after the banquet?

COUZAN: After the banquet usually there's a ball...

PAULETTE: And after the ball is over?

COUZAN: The newlyweds go home together.

PAULETTE: What about the mystery? There's an awesome and delectable mystery to it.

COUZAN: *(Staggered)* Bless my soul! Who told you that?

PAULETTE: *(Crying out and crossing L)* So it *was* true! There is one, and I don't know what it is.

COUZAN: Paulette, listen to me.

PAULETTE: No, no, you blurted it out! Besides, for the past five weeks, I've been thinking: marriage can't merely consist of sleeping next to one another like a couple of hamsters. There's got to be something more! In which case, I've been cheated, wouldn't you say?

COUZAN: Paulette!

PAULETTE: For pity's sake, tell me what I've been cheated of.

COUZAN: *(Most embarrassed)* Why, you see... I've forgotten... It was so long ago, you know!

PAULETTE: Really? In that case, I'll ring for the cook... she's been married only three years, she can't have forgotten so soon. *(She heads U.)*

COUZAN: *(Quickly stopping her)* Don't do that! All we need is to have the servants in on this.

PAULETTE: *(Crossing D and sitting L of the table)* You see, you haven't forgotten. *(Weeping)* Oh, I'm so unhappy!

MME DUPONT: *(Entering U C, her face still smeared with paint)* Oof! What a day!

PAULETTE: Ah! Mama! If you only knew! *(Stopping)* Oh! what have you got all over your face?

MME DUPONT: My face?

COUZAN: Yes, you look like a redskin on the warpath.

MME DUPONT: Ah? I know...my husband did that with a palette full of paints.

COUZAN: You had a brush with the law?

MME DUPONT: Oh, the poor dear, to think I accused him and beat him up. But if that were all!

PAULETTE: No, that isn't all. Mama, prepare yourself for a horrible shock: My husband isn't my husband and I'm not his wife!

MME DUPONT: Eh? Who told you that?

PAULETTE: *(Forcefully)* My little sister.

MME DUPONT: *(Aghast)* Your little sister?

COUZAN: *(Startled)* Oh, for heaven's sake!

MME DUPONT: That little limb of Satan told you that?

PAULETTE: Yes, Mama, she's the one who opened my eyes.

MME DUPONT: *(Aside)* And to think I never let her read anything but fairy tales, and expurgated at that!

PAULETTE: Monsieur de Trivelin doesn't love me, he's never loved me.

MME DUPONT: Oh, as far as that goes, he's not up to it! Monsieur de Trivelin is a loser and I intend to give him his walking papers no later than tonight.

COUZAN: *(In an undertone)* She looks like an Apache scalping her foe.

MME DUPONT: What did you say?

# ACT THREE

COUZAN: Nothing, Big Chief!

MME DUPONT: In three months' time, my daughter will be divorced.

PAULETTE: *(Approving)* Oh! Good!

MME DUPONT: *(While removing her hat, which she places on the furniture L of the U C door)* And in another year, she will be remarried.

PAULETTE: *(Crossing to C)* To anybody at all, so long as he teaches me the awesome mystery.

MME DUPONT: You will wed La Baule, we've arranged it with him. *(She crosses D R.)*

PAULETTE: Fine. I don't love him, but that doesn't matter.

COUZAN: But for mercy's sake! You're about to commit an irreparable wrong! And as your godfather, I have the right…

MME DUPONT: To keep your mouth shut.

COUZAN: *(To* PAULETTE*)* But your husband adores you, I give you my word!

MME DUPONT: You mean he adores another woman.

PAULETTE: *(Crying out)* Eh?

MME DUPONT: Yes, my child…another woman… at this very moment your father and La Baule are busy collecting proof positive to charge him with his infamous behavior.

PAULETTE: *(Throwing herself in her mother's arms and weeping)* Another woman! He loves another woman!

MME DUPONT: There, there, don't cry, my precious. The villain isn't worth tears from an angel like you.

PAULETTE: *(Weeping)* Ah! Mama!…

MME DUPONT: Tell Ernestine to go out and buy me some turpentine.

PAULETTE: Yes, Mama!

MME DUPONT: And when the proof I'm waiting for arrives, I'll expect to find you in your room.

PAULETTE: Yes, Mama. *(On her way out)* Oh! I hate him now, I hate him! *(She exits D R.)*

COUZAN: Oh really! My dear lady, what do you mean, another woman?

MME DUPONT: I mean that Count de Trivelin keeps a concubine like Louis XIV.

COUZAN: A concubine like Louis XIV?

MME DUPONT: A mistress. The gentleman can't make a peep in his own house, because he's shouting himself hoarse somewhere else. We had him followed, and he went to a floozy's!

COUZAN: *(Gleefully)* Are you sure?

MME DUPONT: Didn't I say he was followed?

COUZAN: *(Rubbing his hands together)* So he went there at last!

MME DUPONT: You approve?

COUZAN: Of course I do, I was the one who sent him.

MME DUPONT: How's that, monsieur! ...Do you get a commission?

COUZAN: Madame Dupont, it was the only way to bring back the poor boy's voice!

ERNESTINE: *(Entering U C and announcing)* Monsieur La Baule!

*(LA BAULE appears. ERNESTINE exits.)*

MME DUPONT: Well, where's the proof?

# ACT THREE

LA BAULE: *(Carrying* DE TRIVELIN *clothes and coming D C)* Here it is!

MME DUPONT: At last!

LA BAULE: It wasn't easy! …I risked life and limb to get it…I nabbed your son-in-law stark naked in that creature's room and made off with his clothes. Here they are!

MME DUPONT: *(Taking the clothes)* Bravo!

COUZAN: A fine way to behave!

LA BAULE: Beg pardon?

MME DUPONT: Don't pay any attention to this nobody…La Baule, you have deserved well of your mother-in-law-to-be. *(She indicates the clothes.)*

LA BAULE: So I'm the first in line!

MME DUPONT: More than ever! *(She puts the clothes on the table.)*

COUZAN: Excuse me! You are forgetting one little detail. Monsieur de Trivelin has until midnight to become his wife's husband. He will be back.

LA BAULE: Not a chance. I've had him locked up.

COUZAN & MME DUPONT: Eh?

LA BAULE: I denounced him to the police as the Vincennes sex fiend!

MME DUPONT: Bravo!

LA BAULE: And you know the efficiency of French law: If they let him go before the month is up, he'll be lucky.

COUZAN: *(Indignant)* How could you do such a thing?

LA BAULE: I'm proud of it!

MME DUPONT: I'm mad about this boy. *(She kisses him.)* And now I'm going to go to my daughter and apprise her of the full extent of her unhappiness.

COUZAN: Madame Dupont, listen to me.

MME DUPONT: Oh, go fly a kite, you! *(She exits D R.)*

COUZAN: For pity's sake! *(He exits following* MME DUPONT.*)*

LA BAULE: *(Alone)* De Trivelin, you're done for! Ha ha! Slap me, will you! I'll make off with your wife. *(Struck with an idea)* Damn! I forgot to bring my bouquet! I'd better phone a florist to send a bunch of roses! Ah! Paulette! Paulette! How happy we shall be together! *(He exits D L.)*

DE TRIVELIN: *(Alone, enters and speaks into the wings. He is still wearing clothes over his pajamas.)* Home at last… Ah! Paulette, my Lélette! Now I shall be your husband! I shall carry you far away from your loathsome family, just as soon as I've changed clothes… Ah! Saint Anthony of Padua, patron saint of missing objects, if only you could bring me back the lightweight suit that scum La Baule stole from me… *(Noticing the clothes on the table)* What do I see? A miracle! Here it is! *(He picks up the clothes.)* Thank you, Saint Anthony. *(Voices offstage)* Someone's coming! I'll get dressed in the next room. *(He exits D L.)*

*(*FRONTIGNAC *appears U C,* DUPONT'S *clothes under his arm.* ERNESTINE *follows him.)*

ERNESTINE: I repeat, monsieur, the master is not at home yet.

FRONTIGNAC: I'm perfectly aware of that fact, indeed I am.

ERNESTINE: The master is in court.

FRONTIGNAC: Is that so? …Do you know where your boss really is? He's in the pokey! He's the Vincennes sex fiend!

ERNESTINE: Monsieur Dupont?

# ACT THREE

FRONTIGNAC: Yes, he's a notorious pervert! Here are his clothes, I've brought them back. *(He lays them on the table where* DE TRIVELIN's *clothes had been.)*

ERNESTINE: So he's the sex fiend? Well, I'm not at all surprised. He's got shifty little eyes…

FRONTIGNAC: Skip it! …I'm off to see a lawyer…

*(They disappear U C.)*

LA BAULE: *(Entering D L)* That's done! There'll be a bouquet here in an hour, an engagement bouquet.

MME DUPONT: *(Entering, followed by* PAULETTE *and* COUZAN*)* Come, my child, come!

PAULETTE: La Baule has brought proof that my husband is cheating on me? Where is it?

MME DUPONT: Right here. *(She picks up the coat.)*

LA BAULE: Irrefutable proof. Monsieur de Trivelin's own clothes…

MME DUPONT: *(Handing the coat to* PAULETTE*)* While he romps in the nude with a courtesan!

PAULETTE: Oh, the wretch! *(Looking at the coat)* But these aren't Robert's clothes, surely!

COUZAN & MME DUPONT: *(Together)* Eh?

MME DUPONT: *(Taking the coat)* Not his clothes?

LA BAULE: I beg your pardon! I took them from him myself chez Zézé!

MME DUPONT: Chez Zézé?

LA BAULE: Chez Zézé! And I've examined his wallet… Look, in the pocket.

MME DUPONT: *(Who has taken the wallet)* Here it is. Oh, my goodness!… *(Opening the wallet and seeing the visiting cards)* Magistrate of the Ninth District Court… Benjamin Dupont!

COUZAN, LA BAULE, & MME DUPONT: Huh?

COUZAN: *(Aside)* Ah! that's a good one!

MME DUPONT: These are my husband's clothes.

LA BAULE: *(Aside, dumbfounded)* Damn it all!

MME DUPONT: Then *he* was the one romping with a courtesan!

PAULETTE: Mama!

(COUZAN, *who is next to* PAULETTE, *makes her keep still.*)

MME DUPONT: *(Furious)* Ah! Every time you help me nab my son-in-law, I run into my husband. *(She throws the coat in his face.)*

LA BAULE: I swear I can't understand it. It must be magic.

MME DUPONT: Is that so! And you say the hussy to whose flat you brought me is named Zézé?

LA BAULE: Yes, she's a painter…

MME DUPONT: The one who paints with her feet?

LA BAULE: Of course not. With her hands.

MME DUPONT: Then she's not an amputee?

LA BAULE: An amputee, her? Ha! I can guarantee she's fully equipped.

MME DUPONT: *(Uttering a cry of rage)* Ah! Ah! And just the other day Monsieur Dupont swore that she was old and handicapped!

LA BAULE: *(Aside)* Holy Moses!

MME DUPONT: *(Crossing L)* O ye gods and little fishes! I'm beginning to see the light.

LA BAULE: Madame Dupont! Listen to me.

# ACT THREE

MME DUPONT: What for? I have a feeling a terrible tragedy is going to take place in Paris today! *(She exits U C, carrying off her hat from the furniture near the door.)*

LA BAULE: Madame Dupont!

PAULETTE: *(To* LA BAULE*)* Explain what's going on!...

LA BAULE: *(Putting the coat back on the table)* It's magic, Paulette, my dear, it s black magic!... *(Crying out)* Oh God!

PAULETTE: Now what is it?

LA BAULE: *(Louder)* Oh God, oh God!

PAULETTE: Tell me!

LA BAULE: If your father was in the nude chez Zézé, they must have arrested him!

PAULETTE: Huh?

COUZAN: *(Aside, laughing)* Dupont arrested!...

LA BAULE: I've had my father-in-law tossed in the clink! I'll run over to the station house. I've had my father-in-law tossed in the clink! *(He exits quickly U C.)*

COUZAN: Well, now you see I was right. Your husband was being slandered.

PAULETTE: Maybe, so far as this Zézé is concerned, but if he's in love with some other woman, the name doesn't matter.

COUZAN: But I repeat...

PAULETTE: *(Cutting him off)* Please, godfather, let's have no more talk about that gentleman. I have no wish to know anything about him.

*(*DE TRIVELIN *appears.)*

DE TRIVELIN: *(Entering U L, without seeing* PAULETTE. *He is now wearing his own clothes.)* Why, Couzan! Good afternoon!

COUZAN: *(Crossing to him)* My dear Trivelin! *(Whisper)* Well, how did my method work?

DE TRIVELIN: *(Whisper)* Like a charm! I can guarantee results.

COUZAN: *(Very low whisper)* At last! It was about time! *(Indicating* PAULETTE.*)* She is over there! *(Aloud)* I shall leave you two alone. You have a lot to talk about. *(He goes to the door UL.)*

DE TRIVELIN: Indeed we do!

PAULETTE: Talk, monsieur and I? You are mistaken, godfather, we have nothing to say to one another. *(She crosses R.)*

DE TRIVELIN: *(Coming D C)* Nothing to say to one another?

COUZAN: *(Coming D L)* Paulette!

PAULETTE: Well, yes, I do have this to say: "I have learned the facts about you, monsieur, and I have been cheated!"

DE TRIVELIN: Ah! Her old harpy of a mother!

PAULETTE: Go ahead! Insulting my mother was the next step.

DE TRIVELIN: Paulette, for pity's sake...

PAULETTE: Tomorrow I am filing for divorce.

DE TRIVELIN: Divorce?

PAULETTE: And I'm marrying La Baule.

DE TRIVELIN: That idiot?...

PAULETTE: Why not? At least he won't shortchange me. *(She heads for the door U R.)*

DE TRIVELIN: Paulette! Listen to me!

PAULETTE: Too late! So you're finally in the mood?

DE TRIVELIN: *(Forcefully)* Yes! Oh yes!

## ACT THREE

PAULETTE: Well, I'm not! *(She exits D R and locks herself in.)*

DE TRIVELIN: She locked herself in! Ah! Blast it to hell! That's the limit!

COUZAN: Won't you try and reason with her?

DE TRIVELIN: What's the use? She won't listen to anyone but her mother or her father. *(Struck by an idea.)* Oh! Her father! ...Of course! He alone can save me! *(Going U C; in a melodramatic tone.)* Curse you, La Baule, you haven't won her yet! *(To himself)* I've got my secret weapon—Rembrandt! *(He goes to the door U L.)*

COUZAN: What are you going to do?

DE TRIVELIN: *(Dramatically)* Fire my last bullet! *(He exits U L.)*

COUZAN: Poor fellow. He must be losing his mind!

*(*DUPONT *appears U C, entering cautiously backwards; he is dressed as a traffic cop, with a white billy club in his belt. Both the uniform and the cap are too large.)*

COUZAN: Oh! The police! *(Recognizing* DUPONT, *who turns around)* Dupont!

DUPONT: Not so loud. Where is my wife?

COUZAN: In her room.

DUPONT: Oh! My friend, I'm crushed, annihilated! If you only knew what I've been through... Zézé! Zézé... was married! *(He falls into a chair L of the table.)*

COUZAN: No!

DUPONT: And I was nabbed by her husband the camel jockey.

COUZAN: Really?

DUPONT: That's not all...I was arrested in her flat in my underwear...and do you know who they thought I was?

COUZAN: The sex fiend…

DUPONT: *(Rising)* How do you know that?

COUZAN: Never mind, I'll tell you later.

DUPONT: All right. Once I got to the station I tried to get myself identified. I said, I'm Dupont…his honor, good old Judge Dupont.

COUZAN: And they let you go?

DUPONT: Oh sure! There were some cops there I had once fined for police brutality…they recognized me… but they pretended not to, the bastards… Oh, my friend! The rubber hose they used on me! It would turn you off watering the lawn for the rest of your life.

COUZAN: But I thought the third degree was illegal?

DUPONT: I thought so too, but they've got some left over they want to use up! Anyway, I was able to escape, thanks to this uniform, which one of the less ferocious officers was willing to lend me.

COUZAN: Aha!

DUPONT: But that's not all. Just in front of the opera house, I ran into a traffic jam… A big hulking traffic cop catches sight of me in my getup *(He indicates the white billy club.)* and shouts, "Hey! Are you the new man? It's about time! Get to work or I'll kick your ass."

COUZAN: *(Laughing)* It's not your day.

DUPONT: Well, I couldn't answer back, so for fifteen minutes, under the cop's watchful eye, I conducted traffic… *(He pulls out the white billy club and performs traffic-conducting movements.)* You know, it's not as easy as you'd think. There's a special flick of the wrist you have to pick up. *(He does the gesture.)* I got rather good at it. *(Putting the billy club back in his belt)* I was wondering where it would all end, when suddenly I

# ACT THREE

heard the shout, "Stop, thief!" and when the cop took off, I made tracks and here I am.

COUZAN: *(Laughing)* That's the first time a judge was saved by a thief!

DUPONT: That's why I intend to acquit him! Now I've got to change out of this outfit. *(He indicates the uniform.)*

COUZAN: Here are your clothes. La Baule brought them back. *(He points to the clothes on the table.)*

DUPONT: La Baule!

COUZAN: He brought them from Zézé's, thinking they were De Trivelin's.

DUPONT: And my wife saw them.

COUZAN: And recognized them...

DUPONT: Oh! Now I'm in for it!

COUZAN: That's not all! La Baule was the one who got you arrested, thinking he was getting rid of your son-in-law.

DUPONT: Huh? I owe that to La Baule as well?

COUZAN: Yes. If I were in your shoes, I'd be pretty careful before I let such a bungler into my family...

DUPONT: You're telling me! Ha! He'll pay me for that in one lump sum!

COUZAN: Bravo! But first go and change your clothes, your wife may come in any minute now.

DUPONT: Right you are... Give me a hand... *(He exits U R, followed by COUZAN.)*

*(As they disappear, DE TRIVELIN appears, bearing in his arms FRONTIGNAC's clothes which he had worn earlier. He rings.)*

DE TRIVELIN: *(After ringing, goes and places Frontignac's clothes on the table)* And Dupont isn't back yet.

ERNESTINE: *(Entering U C)* Monsieur rang?

DE TRIVELIN: *(Indicating the clothes on the table)* Take these clothes to Monsieur Frontignac at the Grand Hotel right away!

ERNESTINE: Yes, monsieur.

(DE TRIVELIN *reexits L.*)

ERNESTINE: *(Alone, grumbling)* Just when I'm about to set the table, I have to go the Grand Hotel…

(ERNESTINE *picks up the clothes from the table. At that moment* MME DUPONT *appears and sees her doing so.*)

MME DUPONT: Ernestine! Who gave you permission to touch those clothes?

ERNESTINE: But, Madame…

MME DUPONT: *(Cutting her off)* Put them back on that table and make it snappy.

ERNESTINE: But…

MME DUPONT: But me no buts. Do as I tell you and don't answer back.

ERNESTINE: Very good, madame. *(She lays the clothes on the table.)*

MME DUPONT: I forbid you to touch them, you hear me? They are exhibit A in the case against Monsieur Dupont.

ERNESTINE: *(Aside)* The sex fiend!

MME DUPONT: Has Monsieur Dupont come home yet?

ERNESTINE: I don't know, madame.

MME DUPONT: All right then, take a look in his study.

ERNESTINE: Go in a room alone with the master? I'd be too scared.

# ACT THREE

MME DUPONT: Scared of what?

ERNESTINE: Why, scared he might molest me!

MME DUPONT: Eh?

(DUPONT, *now wearing his own clothes, appears U R.*)

ERNESTINE: *(Seeing* DUPONT *enter, utters a cry)* Ah! There he is! *(She runs out U C.)*

DUPONT: What's got into the girl?

MME DUPONT: What's got into her, monsieur, is that the rumor of your debauchery and orgies has reached even her ears.

DUPONT: *(Coming D)* The rumor of my debauchery and orgies?

MME DUPONT: Defendant Benjamin Dupont, you deceived me earlier today, just as you did the day before yesterday: Zézé is not a handicapped old woman, Zézé does not paint with her feet! Zézé is your concubine!

DUPONT: *(Indignant)* Lies! Falsehoods! I am innocent. *(He crosses L.)*

MME DUPONT: All the evidence is against you!

DUPONT: So what? In my long career on the bench, I have sentenced enough people on nothing but circumstantial evidence to know what that's worth.

MME DUPONT: Order! Order! I have more than circumstantial evidence! I have proof!

DUPONT: Proof?

MME DUPONT: These clothes. *(She picks the coat off the table.)*

DUPONT: What clothes?

MME DUPONT: Your clothes, monsieur, which La Baule seized at that creature's flat.

DUPONT: *(Taking the coat)* Why, these aren't mine!

MME DUPONT: Is that so! Then what about the wallet?

DUPONT: The wallet?

MME DUPONT: There in the pocket. Doesn't it belong to you either? What about the calling cards inside?

DUPONT: *(Who has pulled out the wallet and read the calling cards)* Frontignac, camel dealer. *(He shows them to* MME DUPONT.*)* Frontignac.

MME DUPONT: *(Uttering a cry of surprise and grabbing the wallet)* Huh?

DUPONT: *(Aside, gleefully)* Frontignac's clothes!

MME DUPONT: And yet I'm not nearsighted.

DUPONT: *(Handing the coat back to her)* So much for your proof.

MME DUPONT: I saw…saw your wallet with my own eyes. *(She lays the coat and wallet on the table.)*

DUPONT: Aha? Madame Dupont, have you been drinking? This figment of your deranged imagination would suggest it…

MME DUPONT: *(Not listening to him)* La Baule was right. There's magic mixed up in this.

ERNESTINE: *(Entering U R with the policeman's uniform and the white billy club)* Madame!

DUPONT & MME DUPONT: *(Together)* What's the matter?

ERNESTINE: I just found this under your bed. A policeman's uniform.

DUPONT: *(Aside)* Good grief!

MME DUPONT: *(Startled)* A policeman's uniform under my bed?

DUPONT: *(Crossing U, quickly)* Ernestine, put it down there and get out!

# ACT THREE

ERNESTINE: *(Terrified)* Yes, monsieur! *(She lays the uniform on the chair R of the table, and the belt and billy club on the table. Aside, leaving U C, staring at* DUPONT.*)* He looks so lecherous!

MME DUPONT: How did this get there?

DUPONT: *(Awesome)* I intend to explain that myself. *(He takes the billy club.)*

MME DUPONT: Then you know about it?

DUPONT: *(Raising the club and bringing it down in one gesture)* Madame Adélaïde Dupont, maiden name La Branche!...

MME DUPONT: *(Coming closer)* What's got into him?

DUPONT: *(Raising his club)* Order in the court! *(Indignant)* So, while your husband, at the risk of his life, is checking up on your son-in-law, you, you shameless consort, entertain naked traffic cops in your bedroom!

MME DUPONT: I do?

DUPONT: *(Raising the club)* Order, order! You accuse me of keeping a mistress, while in fact you are keeping a mister!

MME DUPONT: Me keep a mister?

DUPONT: Don't deny it! The miserable wretch, caught off guard by my unexpected return, hadn't the time to put his clothes back on.

MME DUPONT: Benjamin, what are you concocting?

DUPONT: Nothing...I uncovered the truth by accident. *(Crossing R)* That's the way we magistrates always discover the truth.

MME DUPONT: But you can't be serious, can you?

DUPONT: And who is your accomplice? A mere traffic cop. Not even a detective.

MME DUPONT: *(Starting to weep)* My God! My God! To think me capable of such a thing?

DUPONT: *(Aside)* I needed a good laugh.

ERNESTINE: *(Entering U C)* Monsieur, there's a policeman here come for his uniform.

DUPONT: *(Aside)* Blast it!

MME DUPONT: *(Crossing U)* Ah! Show him in. Now you'll see!

DUPONT: *(Quickly going U and thrusting himself between* MME DUPONT *and the door)* No, no, I have no desire to see him. I would kill him.

MME DUPONT: Excuse me! I insist!...

DUPONT: And I refuse. *(To* ERNESTINE, *indicating the uniform)* Give that back to him and ten francs as well.

ERNESTINE: *(Taking the uniform and the billy club)* Yes, monsieur! *(She exits U C.)*

MME DUPONT: So that's how things stand? Very well! I'll go and fetch him myself.

DUPONT: *(Stopping her and forcing her to cross U R)* You stay right where you are! I forbid you to see that man ever again, you randy little tart.

MME DUPONT: Benjamin!

DUPONT: *(Very dignified)* I too can pardon a woman taken in adultery, and give ten francs to her lover! However, starting tonight, we shall sleep in separate beds.

MME DUPONT: Separate beds?

DUPONT: *(Sternly)* I have spoken! *(Aside)* That's something gained anyway!

MME DUPONT: *(Aside)* Ooh, there's something fishy about all this.

# ACT THREE

DUPONT: And now, Madame Dupont, to your room and sin no more!

MME DUPONT: *(Aside)* I intend to get to the bottom of this. *(She exits U R.)*

DUPONT: *(Alone, crossing D; gaily)* I do believe I've squelched her for the rest of her life.

*(*ERNESTINE *enters U C.)*

ERNESTINE: Monsieur Frontignac!

DUPONT: Frontignac! I'm not in!

*(*DUPONT *tries to escape D L, just as* FRONTIGNAC *appears U C.)*

FRONTIGNAC: Fine. In that case, I'll wait until you come back.

DUPONT: *(Aside)* Monsieur Zézé!

*(*ERNESTINE *exits U C.)*

FRONTIGNAC: So, they sprung you, did they, my dear sex fiend?

DUPONT: *(Coming to him)* Please, please, I'm not the sex fiend.

FRONTIGNAC: Tsk! tsk…you dirty old man! …My wife wasn't enough for you.

DUPONT: *(Bitterly)* Please, don't go on! …Don't mention that person to me.

FRONTIGNAC: But that's exactly why I came… Hurry up, put on your hat and come with me…

DUPONT: Where to?

FRONTIGNAC: To the Police Inspector…I need your testimony for my divorce.

DUPONT: Excuse me! …I'm not the Dupont you want…I wasn't the one who seduced your wife in Biskra.

FRONTIGNAC: Maybe not, but you are the Dupont I nabbed in her flat in Paris...and that's good enough for me... You made me a cuckold!

DUPONT: Why, I'm a bigger cuckold than you are.

FRONTIGNAC: Huh?

DUPONT: Exactly! You're only her husband! If your wife cheats on you, it's only natural...but I, monsieur, am her lover... *(Bitterly)* It's a hundred times more painful!

FRONTIGNAC: You have a funny way of looking at things! ...Maybe you'd like to sue me for damages?

DUPONT: I'd have every right to do so. When a person marries a floozy like that, he keeps her at home and doesn't put her in circulation.

FRONTIGNAC: Are you coming or not?

DUPONT: I repeat, you'll never get me to be party to such a thing.

FRONTIGNAC: In that case, I shall appeal to your wife and let her make the decision. *(He goes U.)*

DUPONT: *(Stopping him)* Huh? Don't kid around! She'd kill me!

FRONTIGNAC: So what?

DUPONT: So I'd be dead! Frontignac, please, listen to me, camel breeding can't have destroyed all your finer feelings!...

FRONTIGNAC: Who cares! I want a divorce so I can marry my sweetheart!

DUPONT: Are you crazy! You want to remarry! You'll be a worse cuckold with your second wife than you were with the first. It's in your nature!

FRONTIGNAC: You're beginning to get on my nerves! If you refuse to come with me, I'll appeal to your wife.

# ACT THREE

DUPONT: *(Stopping him)* Just a minute! *(Merrily)* There may be a way of settling this... How much do your camels go for at the moment?

FRONTIGNAC: Five hundred francs. Apiece.

DUPONT: Well, suppose I bought ten of them at the going rate?

FRONTIGNAC: *(Scornfully)* Ten camels? Pooh!

DUPONT: A dozen? Two dozen?

FRONTIGNAC: Two dozen camels! ...What's that supposed to be?

DUPONT: Twenty-four camels, that's what! And that's enough humps for any man.

FRONTIGNAC: *(Hesitating)* Twenty-four? ...No, I refuse.

DUPONT: Well, I'll go as high as thirty...I suppose I'll have to open a rental agency! ...There isn't one in Paris for camels...and I'll pay cash!

FRONTIGNAC: It's tempting!

DUPONT: Thirty camels at five hundred francs apiece.

FRONTIGNAC: Sorry, six hundred.

DUPONT: You said five hundred.

FRONTIGNAC: The price just went up!

DUPONT: *(Aside)* You sonuvabitch! *(Aloud)* Let's say six hundred, but not a penny more.

FRONTIGNAC: All right, but on one condition. You have to find a replacement.

DUPONT: A replacement?

FRONTIGNAC: Sure! ...If I'm to get a divorce, my wife has to have a corespondent.

DUPONT: Good grief! *(Aside, struck by an idea)* Oh! De Trivelin, of course... *(He rings.)*

FRONTIGNAC: Only pick out somebody young...after all, you were a bit of a humiliation...

DUPONT: Thanks!

ERNESTINE: *(Appearing U C)* Monsieur rang?

DUPONT: Ask Monsieur de Trivelin to step in here. I have something to say to him.

ERNESTINE: Very good, monsieur. *(She exits D L.)*

DUPONT: I have just the ticket: my son-in-law!

FRONTIGNAC: What's that? Your son-in-law is my wife's lover too?

DUPONT: Yes, and I intend to take advantage of that fact to kick him out right now. But not a word about my involvement.

FRONTIGNAC: Don't worry! ...What a family!

DUPONT: *(To himself, crossing R)* Thirty camels, what am I going to do with thirty camels?

DE TRIVELIN: *(Appearing U L)* You're home at last. *(Uttering a cry at seeing* FRONTIGNAC.*)* Ah!

FRONTIGNAC: *(Also crying out)* Ah!

DE TRIVELIN: *(Aside)* The stranger at Zézé's.

FRONTIGNAC: The man who took my clothes at my wife's place!

DE TRIVELIN: Huh? His wife's place?

DUPONT: *(Severely)* Yes, monsieur, his wife's place! Zézé's real name is Madame Frontignac.

FRONTIGNAC: *(Merrily)* And I'm the husband. That should take the wind out of your sails!

DE TRIVELIN: *(Aside)* Good Lord!

FRONTIGNAC: *(To* DE TRIVELIN*)* Come with me to the Inspector so I can get my divorce.

# ACT THREE

DE TRIVELIN: One moment please! ...I should first like to say a few words to excellent Monsieur Dupont.

FRONTIGNAC: Well, speed it up. Have you got a telephone?

DE TRIVELIN: *(Pointing D L)* In there.

FRONTIGNAC: I'm going to phone my lawyer. *(He exits D L.)*

DUPONT: *(Aside, watching DE TRIVELIN)* You're going to try and tug at my heartstrings, but you'll just be wasting your time!

DE TRIVELIN: *(Smiling)* Father-in-law dear!...

DUPONT: I am no longer your father-in-law.

DE TRIVELIN: Excuse me, but I still have four hours in which to become my wife's husband.

DUPONT: Oh! Our agreement no longer stands after such behavior! I'm throwing you out!

DE TRIVELIN: *(Smiling)* Not only won't I leave, but I give you ten minutes—you hear—ten minutes, to put me in the clear with Zézé's husband!

DUPONT: What did you say?

DE TRIVELIN: That's not all... Your daughter wants a divorce so she can marry La Baule.

DUPONT: Yes, he's got first place in line.

DE TRIVELIN: Well, I give you another five minutes to kick that gentleman out the door.

DUPONT: *(Sneering)* Ha ha!

DE TRIVELIN: If you choose to delay...

DUPONT: Oh no, let me have a good laugh. If I choose to delay?

DE TRIVELIN: I shall go to Madame Dupont.

DUPONT: Good idea.

DE TRIVELIN: Madame Dupont's a decent woman!

DUPONT: Indeed she is.

DE TRIVELIN: And I shall say one word, and one alone.

DUPONT: What word?

DE TRIVELIN: *(Forcefully)* Rembrandt!

DUPONT: *(Starting)* Huh!

DE TRIVELIN: Rembrandt! And if she asks for explanations…

DUPONT: *(Aside)* He knows everything!

DE TRIVELIN: *(Continuing)* I shall give her a few unpublished details about that Dutch master and his clandestine love affairs.

DUPONT: *(Melting and taking him in his arms)* Trivelin, my boy, my dear friend… You wouldn't do that!

DE TRIVELIN: Yes, I would! So that's what you call encouraging women in the arts?

DUPONT: It's blackmail then?

DE TRIVELIN: No, just an ugly threat.

DUPONT: Listen, Robert, my beloved son-in-law, if one of us is to be sacrificed, I suggest it be you… You're still young, you have your future ahead of you… You can start life afresh, but I'm over the hill.

DE TRIVELIN: This is delicious!

DUPONT: And, besides, my wife would kill me. You would have my death on your conscience.

DE TRIVELIN: Sure, sure!

DUPONT: For heaven's sake, what do you want me to tell Frontignac?

DE TRIVELIN: Whatever you like. Just find another guilty party. Zézé's got plenty of lovers.

# ACT THREE

DUPONT: I'm sure of that, but I haven't anyone at my disposal.

GONTRAN: *(Entering D L)* Here I am, father-in-law dear!

DUPONT: *(Annoyed)* Des Barbettes…I'm busy… What do you want?…

GONTRAN: *(Coming D L)* I've brought you the affidavit—you know?

DUPONT: What affidavit?

GONTRAN: Didn't you ask me to bring you proof attesting to my ability to have a mistress…so that Lise wouldn't be cheated the way her sister was.

DUPONT: Oh yes.

DE TRIVELIN: What, you told him about it too?

GONTRAN: Here it is!

DUPONT: *(Crying out)* Zézé's handwriting!

DE TRIVELIN: Zézé!

GONTRAN: Yes, she was the one I went to. Do you know her?

DUPONT: *(Quickly)* Only by reputation.

DE TRIVELIN: *(Aside)* The whole family's had her.

DUPONT: *(Gleefully reading)* I certify that the aforesaid Gontran des Barbettes has been my lover!… *(Undertone to* DE TRIVELIN.*)* We're saved!

DE TRIVELIN: *(Undertone)* Right!

GONTRAN: You're satisfied?

DUPONT: Ecstatic… However, Des Barbettes, my boy, you won't get my daughter.

GONTRAN: What's that?

DUPONT: *(Sternly)* I would never give my child to a gadabout who cheats on her during the engagement period. Aren't you ashamed?

GONTRAN: *(Dumbfounded)* But you yourself demanded...

DUPONT: It was a trap to test your fidelity.

GONTRAN: A trap?

DE TRIVELIN: *(Aside)* Poor boy!

GONTRAN: Monsieur Dupont...I prefer to tell you everything. I have not cheated on Lise... This affidavit is false.

DUPONT: *(Incredulous)* Sure it is! This paper will be instantly put in the hands of Zézé's husband, for she happens to be married.

GONTRAN: You would do such a thing?

DUPONT: Yes, monsieur.

GONTRAN: *(Aside)* Couzan's magic word to my rescue. *(Aloud, lifting a finger and in a threatening tone.)* Stop! No, monsieur, you will do no such thing, because I shall prevent you with one word and one word only.

DUPONT: And what word is that?

GONTRAN: *(Forcefully)* Rembrandt!

DE TRIVELIN: *(Aside)* That's a good one!

DUPONT: *(Aside)* He knows everything too!

GONTRAN: *(As before, louder)* Rembrandt!

DUPONT: Be quiet, you wretched boy, be quiet...

GONTRAN: It works. *(Aloud)* Give me back that paper at once or else...

DUPONT: But...

GONTRAN: Rem...

# ACT THREE

DUPONT: *(Hushing him)* Be quiet, there it is. *(He gives it to him.)*

GONTRAN: Thank you...I was to have married Lise in no less than a month...I shall marry her in two weeks' time.

DUPONT: I beg your pardon?

GONTRAN: Rem...

DUPONT: *(Putting a hand over his mouth)* Be quiet, I consent... Ah! Now I'm in a nice fix! *(To* DE TRIVELIN, *cordially)* I'll have to resort to you, after all.

DE TRIVELIN: Sorry! Rembrandt!

DUPONT: Good grief! *(Turning to* GONTRAN*)* Des Barbettes, listen to me.

GONTRAN: Rembrandt!

DUPONT: *(Pleading)* My friends!

DE TRIVELIN & GONTRAN: *(In unison, wagging a finger at him and backing out)* Rem-bur-andt! *(They leave U L.)*

DUPONT: Ah! The cutthroats, they've got me!

FRONTIGNAC: *(Entering D L)* Well, have you finished your little chat? Where's your son-in-law?

DUPONT: Listen, Frontignac. Another twenty camels if you give up this divorce.

FRONTIGNAC: Never!

DUPONT: My son-in-law knows my secret. He's blackmailing me.

FRONTIGNAC: What a family!

DUPONT: At least give me time to find somebody else, say a week from now.

FRONTIGNAC: I give you five minutes and not a moment longer.

DUPONT: *(Aside)* Then I'm doomed!

LA BAULE: *(Entering U C and coming D C)* Oh! My dear Monsieur Dupont! I've found you at last... *(Greeting* FRONTIGNAC*)* Monsieur!

DUPONT: *(Furious)* Ah, there you are! What disaster are you hatching now?

LA BAULE: Don't give me a hard time! If you only knew how sorry I am.

DUPONT: You think sorry will do it? Every problem I've had since this morning I owe to you.

LA BAULE: *(Pleading)* Monsieur Dupont...

DUPONT: Just yesterday I had a mistress I adored...

LA BAULE: *(Quickly)* Don't fret about her, she's not worthy of you.

DUPONT: Then you know Zézé?

LA BAULE: Dear me, yes! Doesn't everybody? Look, I'll bet that this gentleman here... *(He indicates* FRONTIGNAC.*)* whom I don't even know...has had her too.

FRONTIGNAC: On occasion.

LA BAULE: You see! Don't you know her nickname is Measles?

FRONTIGNAC: Measles?

DUPONT: Why?

LA BAULE: Because everyone's had her!

DUPONT: And you too...you've done your share of measling?

LA BAULE: For over a year... She used to call me Fragonard. In fact, here's her photograph. I forgot to return it just now.

# ACT THREE

DUPONT: *(Gleefully)* Give it here! Give it here! *(Aloud. Reading:)* "To my sweet little La Baule alias Fragonard, from his sugar-plum fairy... Zézé." *(Aside)* Saved!

FRONTIGNAC: Let me see that!

DUPONT: *(Crossing to* FRONTIGNAC*)* With pleasure!

(FRONTIGNAC *pockets the photograph.*)

LA BAULE: Excuse me... won't you return it...

FRONTIGNAC: After the divorce.

LA BAULE: The divorce?

DUPONT: Ah, that's right, you don't know this gentleman. *(Introducing them)* La Baule—Frontignac, camel dealer and Zézé's husband.

LA BAULE: *(Staggered)* Zézé's husband!

FRONTIGNAC: *(Merrily)* In other words, Mister Measles! *(To* DUPONT.*)* My dear sex fiend, you are now cleared of any responsibility.

LA BAULE: Monsieur, listen to me...

FRONTIGNAC: There's no need to come with me to the Inspector. Your photograph is sufficient grounds for divorce. See you soon. *(He exits U C.)*

LA BAULE: Ah! The nerve! ...My dear father-in-law...

DUPONT: *(Indignant)* Me, your father-in-law? Never! Give my daughter to a man who's had measles for over a year!

LA BAULE: Damn and blast!

DUPONT: *(Noticing* FRONTIGNAC's *clothes on the table)* Ah! He forgot his suit. *(Picking up* FRONTIGNAC's *clothes.)* Hey! Frontignac, your clothes!

(*He exits U C.* LA BAULE *falls into the chair L of the table and starts to cry.*)

LA BAULE: *(Alone, weeping)* Oh dear, oh dear, oh dear!

PAULETTE: *(Entering D R)* What's this? La Baule, you're still crying even though you're going to marry me?

LA BAULE: Your barbarian of a father has reneged on his promise.

PAULETTE: Why?

LA BAULE: Because I've had measles.

PAULETTE: Is that all? Well, in that case, I shall remake the promise.

LA BAULE: O rapture!

PAULETTE: And you can tell my father I did it!

LA BAULE: I'm off, Paulette, my love, I'm off! *(Exits, shouting)* She's remade the promise, father-in-law! *(He disappears U C.)*

PAULETTE: *(Alone)* Yes, I will marry him, if only to infuriate Monsieur de Trivelin.

*(DE TRIVELIN appears U L.)*

DE TRIVELIN: Alone! At last!

PAULETTE: You again, monsieur! I shall leave the room to you. *(She takes a step towards her room.)*

DE TRIVELIN: *(Stopping her)* Oh! Not before you've heard me out this time, my love!

PAULETTE: His love! He dares call me his love, when he's never loved me.

DE TRIVELIN: Not loved you?

PAULETTE: If you had loved me, monsieur, I should know that famous awesome and delectable mystery, I should know love.

DE TRIVELIN: But you don't know...

PAULETTE: *(Interrupting him)* You're telling me? I've been married for over a month and I still don't know anything!

# ACT THREE

DE TRIVELIN: That's not what I mean! You see, it's all the fault of the customs inspector...

PAULETTE: What customs inspector?

DE TRIVELIN: That beastly customs inspector who burst into our compartment on the train to Brussels.

PAULETTE: I don't see the connection.

DE TRIVELIN: You don't see it, but, believe me, it's there.

PAULETTE: In other words, if the Belgian customs had been abolished the night before our wedding, I should have been your wife this past month.

DE TRIVELIN: There you have it!

PAULETTE: Indeed? Monsieur, do you take me for a goose, with your stories about customs inspectors?

DE TRIVELIN: Paulette! Please! I realize that when I tell you something like that, I must sound like an idiot...

PAULETTE: You certainly do! *(She crosses R.)*

DE TRIVELIN: *(Catching up to her in front of the table)* Because you can't understand. *(Taking her in his arms)* But if I never loved you, would I be so upset at the thought of losing you?

PAULETTE: *(Trying to get free)* Let go of me! Let go of me!

DE TRIVELIN: If I hadn't adored you, would I be clasping you in my arms like this?

PAULETTE: *(In a fainter voice)* Let go of me, I said!

DE TRIVELIN: Would I be kissing you like this? *(He kisses her.)*

PAULETTE: *(Very quiet)* I don't love you any more.

DE TRIVELIN: There, there!

PAULETTE: *(Very quiet)* Not a bit, not a bit!

(LA BAULE *appears U C.*)

LA BAULE: *(Crying out)* Ah!

PAULETTE: *(Aside, pulling free)* La Baule!

DE TRIVELIN: What! Is he still here?

LA BAULE: *(Stepping forward with dignity)* Monsieur, I forbid you to touch this lady, even with a glance. She is my betrothed.

DE TRIVELIN: Betrothed to a tub of lard like you?

LA BAULE: And the proof that we are betrothed is that I am going to kiss her before your very eyes.

*(LA BAULE kisses PAULETTE.)*

PAULETTE: *(Slapping him)* How dare you!

LA BAULE: *(Crying out)* You too!

PAULETTE: *(Throwing herself in her husband's arms)* It's you I adore!...

DE TRIVELIN: *(Leading her off)* Come, darling!

*(He draws her into the room D R and locks the door.)*

LA BAULE: *(Dumbfounded)* There's been a whole family reunion on my cheek. *(Turning around.)* Hey! Where are they going? Into the bedroom! I won't have it! *(Going to the door and trying to open it)* Paulette! Paulette! No answer? *(Going out and coming back C)* Help! Help!

COUZAN: *(Entering U C followed by DUPONT)* What's the matter?

DUPONT: Are you still making a fuss?

LA BAULE: *(In a choked voice)* Paulette is in her bedroom.

DUPONT: So what?

LA BAULE: Locked in with her husband.

COUZAN: *(Aside)* At last!

LA BAULE: Order him out.

DUPONT: Never!

# ACT THREE

MME DUPONT: *(Entering U C, hat on her head, an envelope in her hand)* Monsieur Dupont!

LA BAULE: Ah! Madame Dupont, listen to me.

MME DUPONT: Just a minute. *(To* DUPONT*)* I've just come from Zézé.

DUPONT: *(Aside)* Bloody hell!

MME DUPONT: At the cost of a hundred francs, the floozy's chambermaid gave me the names of all her mistress's lovers since she's lived in Paris. I intended to open this list only in your presence, to confound you. *(She opens the envelope and pulls out a long, long list.)*

DUPONT: *(Aside)* I'm ruined!

MME DUPONT: Here are the names: *(Reading)* El Greco, Titian, Rubens, Van Dyck, Fragonard, Rembrandt, Watteau!

COUZAN: She's not a woman, she's an art museum.

MME DUPONT: But your name isn't here, nor is De Trivelin's.

DUPONT: *(Aside)* I'm saved!

LA BAULE: Madame, listen to me.

MME DUPONT: You have disgracefully slandered my husband and my son-in-law.

LA BAULE: But it's the other thing...Paulette is there in her bedroom...with her husband... They're locked in...

MME DUPONT: *(Delighted)* You don't mean it?

LA BAULE: *(Struck by an idea)* Oh, how stupid of me! *(Going to the door D R and roaring.)* Anything to declare? ...Anything to declare?

DE TRIVELIN: *(Coming out, followed by* PAULETTE, *her eyes downcast)* As a matter of fact, I have to declare that I am now my wife's husband.

LA BAULE: *(Dropping on to the sofa)* Too late!

MME DUPONT: What! Paulette, is this true?

PAULETTE: *(Coming to* MME DUPONT *and throwing herself in her arms)* Yes, Mama!

DUPONT: Come to my arms, son-in-law!

DE TRIVELIN: *(Going to* DUPONT*)* With pleasure, father-in-law!

COUZAN: Didn't I tell you he loved his wife and nobody else?

MME DUPONT: As a reward, you can be godfather to the third one.

DUPONT: You get the bishop! *(To* LA BAULE*)* What do you have to say to that?

LA BAULE: *(Weepily)* No comment! I have nothing to declare!

*(Lineup:* COUZAN, DUPONT, DE TRIVELIN, MME DUPONT, PAULETTE, LA BAULE*)*

### END OF PLAY

www.ingramcontent.com/pod-product-compliance
Lightning Source LLC
Chambersburg PA
CBHW060200050426
42446CB00013B/2925